Preaching the Scriptures
of the
Masses of the
Blessed Virgin Mary

Preaching the Scriptures of the Masses of the Blessed Virgin Mary

David O. Brown, OSM

LITURGICAL PRESS
Collegeville, Minnesota

www.litpress.org

Cover design by Ann Blattner. Artwork by Martin Erspamer, OSB, a monk of Saint Meinrad Archabbey.

ACKNOWLEDGMENTS

The English translation of Psalm Responses, Titles of the Readings, Summaries of the Readings from *Collection of Masses of the Blessed Virgin Mary* © 1987, 1989, International Commission on English in the English in the Liturgy Corporation (ICEL); excerpts from the English translation of *The Roman Missal* © 2010, ICEL. All rights reserved.

Lectionary texts used in this work are taken from *The New American Bible* copyright © 1991, 1986, 1970, by the Confraternity of Christian Doctrine, Washington, DC, and are used by license of the copyright owner. All rights reserved.

Other Scripture texts used in this work are taken from the *New American Bible, revised edition* © 2010, 1991, 1986, 1970 Confraternity of Christian Doctrine, Inc., Washington, DC. All Rights Reserved. No part of this work may be reproduced or transmitted in any form or by any means, electronic or mechanical, including photocopying, recording, or by any information storage and retrieval system, without permission in writing from the copyright owner.

Excerpts from the English translation of the *Catechism of the Catholic Church* for use in the United States of America copyright © 1994, United States Catholic Conference, Inc.—Libreria Editrice Vaticana. English translation of the *Catechism of the Catholic Church: Modifications from the Editio Typica* copyright © 1997, United States Catholic Conference, Inc.—Libreria Editrice Vaticana. Used with Permission.

Excerpts from documents of the Second Vatican Council are from *Vatican Council II: The Basic Sixteen Documents*, by Austin Flannery, OP © 1996 (Costello Publishing Company, Inc.). Used with permission.

1   2   3   4   5   6   7   8   9

Library of Congress Cataloging-in-Publication Data

Brown, David O., Rev.
　　Preaching the scriptures of the masses of the Blessed Virgin Mary / David O. Brown, O.S.M.
　　　　pages　cm
　　Includes bibliographical references.
　　ISBN 978-0-8146-3553-7 — ISBN 978-0-8146-3578-0 (e-book)
　　1. Mary, Blessed Virgin, Saint.　2. Catholic Church. Collectio Missarum de Beata Maria Virgine.　3. Bible—Sermons—Outlines, syllabi, etc.　I. Title.
BX2015.9.M3B76　2013
232.91—dc23

2012051402

In memory of Fra Ignacio Calabui, OSM

CONTENTS

ADVENT SEASON

In Advent, the church celebrates the coming of the Lord. This is illustrated with the first three formulae of the collection. Each helps us to look forward to, and at the same time celebrate, the coming of the Lord. The faith with which we celebrate each of these feasts gives full meaning to the Scripture passages that we use.

1. THE BLESSED VIRGIN MARY, CHOSEN DAUGHTER OF ISRAEL

Exegesis of the First Reading: Genesis 12:1-7

God spoke to our ancestors, to Abraham and his seed for ever.

In this Scripture passage, the Lord instructs Abraham and his wife Sarah: "Go forth from the land of your kinsfolk / and from your father's house to a land that I will show you." In obedience, they "went as the LORD directed." In this passage we find the beginning of salvation history. The movement away from God recounted in the first eleven chapters of the book of Genesis is now reversed. These words describing Abraham's obedience are among the most important words ever spoken in the Scriptures. The obedience of Abraham and Sarah to the Lord initiates the plan of salvation, which will unfold in Moses, the prophets, and the kings and find its embodiment in Israel. The Lord God initiates this change and initiates a covenant with his people, with Mary as an instrument.

Exegesis of the Alternate First Reading: 2 Samuel 7:1-5, 8b-11, 16

The Lord God will give to him the throne of his father, David.

This passage from the book of Samuel about King David reminds us in a very vivid fashion of the difference between the divine and the human. King David had unified the kingdom, made Jerusalem the capital, and was at peace. So, he mused, it was time to do something for God; he would build a temple. Nathan the prophet too saw with human eyes until the Lord spoke to him. Nathan was to remind the king that all he had experienced from being a shepherd to being a soldier to being king was God's work, not David's. And God's work would continue. "Your house and your kingdom shall endure forever before me"—through Mary, the Chosen Daughter of Israel.

Exegesis of the Gospel Reading: Matthew 1:1-17

A genealogy of Jesus Christ, son of David, son of Abraham.

Matthew's gospel traces the ancestry of Jesus back to Abraham. Saint Luke in his gospel will trace the ancestry of Jesus all the way back to Adam. The reason for the difference is that the evangelists were writing to different audiences. Luke will be writing to Christian communities that are, for the most part, Gentiles, who are neither aware of nor concerned so much about the ancestry of Jesus.

Matthew was writing for the Jewish community. His purpose is to show that Jesus is the fulfillment of the prophecies and hopes of Israel, beginning with Abraham continuing through to David. Later in the gospel St. Matthew makes a reference to the family of Jesus but does not mention its Davidic origins. But after the fall of Jerusalem, when the Christians were being criticized, they wanted to show that they belonged and so wanted to assert the Davidic kinship of Jesus.

The inclusion of the four women who contribute to the establishment of the Davidic kinship indicates that salvation is for all, saint and sinner, Jew and Gentile. Thus, the kingdom established by Jesus is not a secret, purely heavenly kingdom but rather one rooted in the human community, of lowly origin and laborious growth, one that has known sin.

Joseph was of this lineage; he was the husband of Mary. "Of Mary was born Jesus who is called the Messiah."

PURPOSE: In the unbroken sweep of salvation history, Mary is a bridge between the old and the new.

SUMMARY: We may want to use the image of a mosaic as a way to illustrate the content of this feast. Each individual stone in a mosaic has its own shape, beauty, and value. One may take it in one's hand and admire its worth and brilliance. When it is placed in its proper place in the final picture, it reveals even more as it contributes to the charm of the whole.

MUSINGS:

1. Revelation began with Adam and Eve, but the tremendous story of salvation and redemption begins to unfold with the choice of Abraham. He was obedient to the will of the Lord God. He was not sure where his journey would lead, but he "went as the LORD directed."

2. This passage gives just a glimpse into the life of Abraham and Sarah, but it shows us how clearly the Lord God chooses his children to carry out his will.

3. When the Lord God said to Abraham that he will make his name great and that all generations will be blessed in him, do we not see here a foretaste of the blessing the Lord God was to bestow on Mary and through her all her children?

4. David's intention was to build a place for the ark of the covenant. The ark was a precious container that held the stones on which the Ten Commandments were inscribed, the staff of Moses with which he had parted the Red Sea, and some of the manna that had sustained them in the desert. All of these were the sign of the presence of God among his people. How much more will the womb of the Chosen Daughter of Israel house the real presence of God among his people?

5. Abraham built an altar to the Lord God to honor the One who appeared to him; we are about to approach our altar to give God all praise.

6. We use only a small portion of the story of Abraham and Sarah, but the whole story is filled with allusions in which we see the place of Mary in the story of salvation.

7. The ark was the repository of the stones of the covenant and the staff of Moses. It was the sign of the presence and power of God on earth. Mary, in her own body, will be the true ark of the covenant, the real sign of God's presence on earth.

8. The passage from the book of Samuel reminds us in a special way of how the Lord God renewed his covenant with his people in David. It was from the descendants of David that the Redeemer would come.

9. These images, pictures, illustrations, and allusions are confirmed when we read the Gospel of Matthew. He was writing to Jewish followers of Jesus about the year 70. As St. Matthew searches the Scriptures to show that Jesus is the Messiah and the fulfillment of the prophecies,

we can conclude with him that Mary is truly "the Chosen Daughter of Israel."

RELATION TO THE EUCHARIST: The story of salvation is the story of faith and it is with faith we approach each celebration.

Sources

Genesis: *Guide for the Christian Assembly: A Background Book of the Mass*, 9 vols., ed. Thierry Maertens and Jean Frisque (Notre Dame, IN: Fides Publishers, 1971), I:132, 160.

The Jerome Biblical Commentary, ed. Raymond E. Brown, Joseph A. Fitzmyer, and Roland E. Murphy (Englewood Cliffs, NJ: Prentice-Hall, 1968), Gen 51; 1 Sam 18; Matt 17.

The Collegeville Bible Commentary, ed. Dianne Bergant and Robert J. Karris (Collegeville, MN: Liturgical Press, 1989), Gen 11:28-29; 12:1-9; 1 Sam 7:17; Matt 1:1-17.

Servants of the *Magnificat*: The Canticle of the Blessed Virgin and Consecrated Life (Rome: General Curia OSM, 1996), 10, 79.

Guide for the Christian Assembly, I:160, 178.

2. THE BLESSED VIRGIN MARY AND THE ANNUNCIATION OF THE LORD

Exegesis of the First Reading: Isaiah 7:10-14, 8:10c

The virgin will conceive.

The church has always considered the Scriptures as a single source whether from the Old or New Testament. So when Isaiah was writing about 755 years before Christ, his writing is considered as though they were speaking of Christ at least indirectly. At the time of Isaiah the kingdom of David had divided into the kingdom of Judah and the kingdom of Israel. Ahaz, the king of Judah, was being besieged by several armies intent on putting an end to his kingdom.

The sign proposed by Isaiah had two goals. The first was concerned with the preservation of Judah in the midst of distress (cf. Isa 7:15, 17). More especially it was concerned with the fulfillment of God's earlier promise to David (2 Sam 7:12-16). Both of these goals would be achieved in the coming of Immanuel, meaning, "With us is God." He would be the ideal king (cf. Isa 9:5-6; 11:1-5). The prophet did not know the full force of his words. The church has always seen the fulfillment of this verse in the birth of Jesus. Some Catholic writers have seen a preliminary and partial fulfillment in the conception and birth of the future King Hezekiah, whose mother, at the time Isaiah spoke, would have been a young, unmarried woman (in Hebrew, *almah*). The Holy Spirit was preparing, however, for another Nativity, which alone would fulfill the terms of Immanuel's mission.

Exegesis of the Gospel Reading: Luke 1:26-38

You will conceive and bear a son.

This passage of Scripture is technically called a "midrash." It is a Hebrew expression that means in addition to the story it is telling on the surface, it also has a deeper meaning that we can find by exploring other passages of Scripture. We will find this literary device frequently in this collection of Masses. The story told here is very familiar to us. Behind and beneath the story, we need to know that the prophet Daniel prophesied that in seventy weeks the kingdom would come (Dan 8:16; 9:21, 24-26). Counting from the appearance of the angel Gabriel to Zechariah in the temple until the birth of Jesus, we have those seventy weeks!

The angel Gabriel was sent from God and uses words that the prophets Zephaniah (3:16) and Zechariah (9:9) had applied to Jerusalem. Gabriel now applies them to Mary. He announces that the privileges of Jerusalem are now transferred to Mary.

The expression "highly favored" or "full of grace" is a special title indicating that Mary was especially favored by God. More than Ruth (2:2, 10, 13) or Esther (2:9, 15, 17; 5:2) or the woman in the book of Proverbs (5:19; 7:5; 18:22; Song 8:10), Mary is filled with the special favor of God.

We might mention that Bl. Pope John Paul II had used the expression "joyful" instead of "hail" as he begins the "Ave." The greeting includes a sense of joy that is missing in the simple word "hail." Here, as in most of the Scriptures, there is more to the message than just the words.

PURPOSE: Between heaven and earth there seems to be an enormous chasm. God chooses to bridge that chasm in a truly marvelous way.

SUMMARY: Scripture scholars tell us that when the gospels were being written, they probably started at the end and worked to the beginning. That is, the original gospel story told of the death and resurrection of Jesus, and then it was expanded to give us an account of his public life. Last to be written down were the infancy narratives filled with details.

MUSINGS:

1. It would be a good guess to say that the church celebrated the birth of the Lord with the Christmas celebrations and then, as they reflected on this mystery, they added this feast of "the Annunciation of the angel to Mary."

2. Our reading from Isaiah today is famous for its prediction that "a virgin shall conceive." Perhaps even more important in this prophecy is the name that was to be given to the child, Immanuel, *God with us*. "God with us" is the most fundamental mystery that we celebrate with this feast.

3. Early in St. John's gospel, he tells us that "the Word became flesh / and made his dwelling among us" (John 1:14). Some older folks remember it was read as the "last gospel," and we were instructed to genuflect. Now, each Sunday as we recite the Creed we bow at the words "was incarnate of the Virgin Mary, and became man." The work of salvation begins with this moment.

4. In the church calendar, the feast of the Annunciation of the Lord is celebrated each year on March 25th. The church also celebrates this event on the Fourth Sunday of Advent, when we use the same reading as we have in this collection.

5. The larger implications of Mary's response to the angel were summarized succinctly at the Second Vatican Council: "The Virgin Mary, who at the message of the angel received the Word of God in her heart and in her body and brought forth life to the world, is acknowledged and honored as truly the mother of God and of the Redeemer" (*Lumen Gentium* 53).

RELATION TO THE EUCHARIST: As we prepare to celebrate the Eucharist, we begin with the realization that it was here, at the Annunciation, that the Word was first made flesh, the very flesh we will receive in Communion.

Sources

Isaiah: *Guide for the Christian Assembly: A Background Book of the Mass*, 9 vols., ed. Thierry Maertens and Jean Frisque (Notre Dame, IN: Fides Publishers, 1971), I:130.

The Catholic Study Bible, ed. Donald Senior (New York: Oxford University Press, 1990), notes to Luke 1:32, 34, 36-37.

3. THE VISITATION OF THE BLESSED VIRGIN MARY

Exegesis of the First Reading: Zephaniah 3:14-18a

The Lord, the King of Israel, is among you.

The prophet Zephaniah very likely lived in Jerusalem. In general, he was a very pessimistic person. He saw the great corruption internally as people neglected their responsibilities. At the same time the kingdom of Assyria is attacking Jerusalem. The Day of Judgment is upon Judah. Still, in the midst of the gloom and doom, there is hope. There is a new king, Josiah. For Zephaniah this is cause for rejoicing. In fact, all Jerusalem is to rejoice; they are to sing and dance. Zephaniah uses the word "rejoice" repeatedly.

The contrast between the gloom of the present and the joy of the future is the real message of this passage.

Exegesis of the Alternate First Reading: Song of Songs 2:8-14

See, my lover comes leaping across the mountains.

Most Catholic scholars consider the book Song of Songs as a story about two lovers. On a deeper level, however, it is the story of the Lord's love for his beloved people. This is its deepest meaning and the point of the whole story. At the same time, the story may also be considered an idealized picture of human love. It delights in the description of young love, so we have the images of the young lover springing across the mountains and hills, peeking through the windows, whispering sweet nothings.

When the lover tells us that the winter is past, he develops the same message that is found in the reading from Zephaniah. There is hope and there is joy.

Later in the book it will speak about the maturity of love and its fidelity that is stronger than death.

Exegesis of the Gospel Reading: Luke 1:39-56

Why should I be honored with a visit from the mother of my Lord?

For this gospel passage we must use the term "midrash" again. It is a Hebrew expression about the various levels of meaning in a story or event. As this story unfolds it uncovers the meaning of many other passages of Scripture as well. In this passage we find many examples of symbolism in the transfer of the ark of the covenant. It is St. Luke's purpose to show us that Jesus is indeed the Messiah whom Malachi and Daniel had foretold in their prophecies. This passage reflects their prophecies and themes. The Messiah was to journey to Jerusalem and to the temple. Mary's own journey is the first stage on that journey.

When the ark of the covenant was transferred to Jerusalem, it was accompanied with displays of great joy, singing and dancing. The ark was the sign of the presence of God among his people. Now Mary is that ark; she is the sign who carries the true presence of God in our midst.

Mary will stay in the house of Zechariah and will be a source of blessing to that house. Elizabeth's words will echo those of King David himself. And Elizabeth's words reflect those of Deborah (Judg 5:2-31) and Judith (Jdt 13:17-18; 15:9-10) as they announced their victories over evil with the help of the Lord.

In the *Magnificat*, Luke continues his comparison between Mary and Israel. Throughout, he puts the words of the psalms and the liturgical hymns of Israel into the mouth of Mary. In a very special way, he relates Mary to the poor. The poor are always a privileged part of the people waiting for the Messiah. Mary is their spokesperson.

In the last part of the *Magnificat*, Mary is identified with Jerusalem, Israel, and the promises made to Abraham, our father in faith. All the hopes and expectations of Israel are found in Mary.

The early Christian community used the vocabulary of the *Magnificat* to express itself. That community also saw itself as the object of the promises made to Abraham, and so the use of the language of gratitude and praise would certainly be the same.

PURPOSE: From the very beginning, being a Christian meant sharing the Good News.

SUMMARY: "Intimate sharing" is the stuff of soap operas and high drama. Here, however, we see the intimate sharing of Mary and Elizabeth is also the stuff of profound theology.

MUSINGS:

1. When people have nothing, no food, no crops, no freedom, when they are completely deprived of everything, they turn to the one unfailing source of help and comfort. They turn to the Lord. The people of Israel were like that. They had suffered persecution, exile, war, and famine. Yet, the Lord would never forget them. They had the temple and the ark. They had the sign of the presence of God among them. So there was hope.

2. As Christians, we find this message of joy, expressed by the prophets, transferred from Jerusalem to Mary. Mary is the one who brings the ark, the sign of the presence of God, to Elizabeth and to the house of Zechariah.

3. While outwardly Elizabeth and Zechariah did not seem to be suffering, all of Palestine was suffering under Roman domination. All were expecting and praying and hoping for the Messiah to come. The gospel of this celebration tells us of that coming. The Messiah comes to Elizabeth, Zechariah, and John the Baptist. There is rejoicing, there is dancing, and we can guess there is singing as well, the *Magnificat*.

4. We sometimes think we have everything, when in fact we have nothing of our own. Whatever we have, we have from the Lord. The Lord comes to us and blesses us and confers on us all the blessings of God's creation. Elizabeth is very direct: Mary is blessed by the Lord.

5. As we celebrate this feast of the Visitation, we remember that it is Mary who brings the Lord to us as she brought the Lord to Elizabeth, Zechariah, and John the Baptist. Mary brings hope.

6. Sometimes people forget the joy and exultation of being young and in love in the springtime. In using the selection from the Song of Songs as we celebrate this Visitation, the church wants us to rejoice with the joy of youth and young love. It is a beautiful thing.

7. As we remember, as we may very well experience again, the joy of being loved, the church reminds us of an even greater love, the love of the Lord for us. It is the love that initiated the incarnation and prompted the journey of Mary to her cousin Elizabeth. How to put it in words? Here the church suggests that we do so by using the words of the Song of Songs.

8. The church uses the gospel account in Advent on December 21 and on the feast of the Visitation on May 31. It is used on the feast of the Assumption and on the feast of the Queenship of Mary, August 22.

RELATION TO THE EUCHARIST: At the visit of Mary, Elizabeth recognized the presence of the Lord. In the company of both, we too attend to the presence of the Lord.

Sources

Zephaniah: *Guide for the Christian Assembly: A Background Book of the Mass*, 9 vols., ed. Thierry Maertens and Jean Frisque (Notre Dame, IN: Fides Publishers, 1971), I:92. (Also used on the Third Sunday of Advent, Cycle C.)
Canticle: Ibid., I:166. (Also used in Advent, December 21.)
Luke: Ibid., I:146.

CHRISTMAS SEASON

During the Christmas season, we remember that Mary stands at the heart of the incarnation.

4. HOLY MARY, MOTHER OF GOD

Exegesis of the First Reading: Galatians 4:4-7

God sent his Son, born of a woman.

In his letter to the Galatians, St. Paul attempts to show that Jesus is the heir to all the promises made to Abraham. It is in Jesus that all those promises would be fulfilled. The birth of Jesus and his mission come from God. They are part of the one divine plan. As we observe the unfolding of this divine plan, we call it "salvation history." The divine plan begins from all eternity. "In the beginning was the Word, /and the Word was with God, /and the Word was God" (John 1:1). It continues unto the fullness of time, when at a specific instant, on our calendar, "God sent his Son, born of a woman" to indicate his human origin. He immediately adds his purpose: "to ransom those [born] under the law."

The Savior, in the words of Paul, is born of a woman for two reasons. First is to emphasize the true, human condition of Jesus. Secondly, he adds the ultimate reason for the incarnation: to bestow the divine life upon us.

John, in his gospel, reveals the same truth with the beautiful words, "And the Word became flesh" (1:14).

Exegesis of the Gospel Reading: Luke 2:15b-19

The shepherds found Mary and Joseph, and the baby lying in the manger.

The words that St. Luke uses in this chapter, "savior," "firstborn," "Lord," already indicate that he is looking forward to and thinking in terms of the paschal mystery. Mary, on her part, reflects on these things because the birth of Jesus signals the beginning, manifestation, and announcement of this same paschal mystery. In the infancy stories Luke is telling us, in anticipation, much of what he will unfold for us, little by little, later in the gospel.

Here in this chapter, as in other places in Luke's gospel, we see words like "amazed" and "praising" used whenever Jesus is revealed. Luke uses these words when he refers to the shepherds. Later he will use these same words when the apostles describe the risen Christ.

We might notice the openness of the shepherds to the message they had received from the angel. Without hesitation they made their way to Bethlehem. We must note a theme that will run through Luke's entire gospel: the poor and the lowly will be singled out for God's favors. Shepherds, in those days, were on the lowest strata of society.

PURPOSE: Mary is not just a chosen and blessed woman. She is the Mother of God.

SUMMARY: We celebrate Mary not only for her place in the life of Jesus but also for her place in the whole mystery of salvation. She was there at the appointed time.

MUSINGS:

1. So often at Christmas time, and even in spite of ourselves, the days are so full that it is possible to be overwhelmed. It is the social season of our society, a time for visiting and exchange of presents. That is why we have this celebration of Holy Mary, the Mother of God. It brings us back to the basics. Jesus is Lord and Savior.

2. Christmas has become a family feast, where members come home, and celebrations are held. It has become a time to remember the happy times of growing up in our family. That is good and can be holy. For us, however, the root, the foundation, the fundamental reality of Christmas is that God has come to earth and Mary is Mother of God.

3. We may think of Christmas as an "epiphany." Etymologically the word epiphany means to make public, to manifest. Christmas makes public the truth that God has become man in Jesus. At the same time, as St. Paul reminds us, this man, Jesus, this Savior, was born of a woman, born of Mary.

4. As we celebrate this "epiphany" of Mary, the Mother of God, amid the abundance of our culture, there may be a special lesson for us to realize that it was to the shepherds, among the poorest of Judah, that the first sight of the Madonna and Child was given.

5. To whom was she made manifest? To whom is she made public? In Luke's gospel, it is to shepherds. In Matthew's gospel, it will be to kings! No one is left out. In John's gospel, it is to the universe. Mark is the pragmatic one. He omits the infancy of Jesus entirely and begins with the public life of Jesus.

6. There are some theologians who speculate it was the birth of Jesus that effected our salvation, not his death. This too is something to think about.

RELATION TO THE EUCHARIST: As we celebrate the passion, death, and resurrection of Jesus in our Eucharist, we also remember that Mary was the instrument of the incarnation.

Sources

Guide for the Christian Assembly: A Background Book of the Mass, 9 vols., ed. Thierry Maertens and Jean Frisque (Notre Dame, IN: Fides Publishers, 1971), I:241, 197.

5. THE BLESSED VIRGIN MARY, MOTHER OF THE SAVIOR

Exegesis of the First Reading: Isaiah 9:1-3, 5-6

A son is given to us.

When the Babylonians had conquered Israel, they actually blinded some of the Hebrew people as they sent them into exile so they were like people who walked in darkness. They were like those who inhabited Sheol, the place of the dead. It was the prophet Isaiah who promised them a light in the form of hope. That hope he promised was embodied in the Messiah, a Child, who is "Wonder-Counselor," "Prince of Peace." His dominion will last forever. He will bring a kingdom of peace.

The book of Isaiah is sometimes called "the fifth gospel" because of the many allusions to Christ. At the time he spoke this prophecy, Isaiah was addressing King Ahaz. At the same time, however, he was speaking of and about the Messiah. Even as he encouraged Ahaz, he was always looking beyond, looking to the final victory of the Messiah.

Some commentators see this prophecy as a liturgical hymn composed for the accession of each of the Davidic kings, including Hezekiah, son of Ahaz. The passage speaks of moving from darkness to light, of rejoicing that the yoke has been lifted and that those who had been taken into exile would return. Leading this procession is the mission of the king.

The church uses this passage at the Midnight Mass on Christmas. At a time when the joy associated with Christmas has too often become something superficial, the words here remind us of what the feast is about. Rejoice and be glad, for a Son is given to us, a Son is born to us, one who will lead us on the way.

Exegesis of the Gospel Reading: Luke 2:1-14

A savior is born for you.

This passage is filled with many references and allusions to other parts of the Scriptures. Whole books have been written about this chapter of Luke's gospel. In the early chapters of his gospel, Luke uses a special literary form called "midrash," which is a combination of historical fact, interpretation, and reflection. Saint Luke is not giving us a history or a biography in our modern sense. He is conveying a message from God, a revelation of God. Here he tells us about the incarnation of the Messiah.

Luke combines several historical imperial Roman edicts into a single one. Again, he is not so much interested in history as he is in presenting the "person" of Jesus to us. Jesus was a historical person, was born in Bethlehem, and had to be counted. At the same time, however, Luke tells us that his birth was surrounded with astounding events.

After the birth of Jesus, the angels announce to shepherds that the Messiah has come. Then the angels sing "Glory." The word "Glory" has a special significance in Scripture. Saint Luke is telling us more than just the words to the angel's song. In the Hebrew Scriptures, this word is always used to point out the special acts of God's providence, for example, when God feeds his people in the desert (Exod 16:7) and again at the dedication of the temple (1 Kgs 8:11). Saint Luke will use this term again at the ascension of Jesus while John in his gospel applies this term to the entire life of Jesus (John 1:14). All were "Glory!"

At the time of the birth of the Lord Jesus, shepherds were poor, despised, and considered untrustworthy. On the other hand, both Abraham and David, ancestors of Jesus, had been shepherds. It is as though Luke is telling us two different things at the same time. First of all, the poor were the first to hear of the birth of the Messiah. Second, the promises made to Abraham and David were now fulfilled. Luke uses the word "fulfilled" eight times in the first two chapters of his gospel!

The angels tell the shepherds that a Savior will be found in Bethlehem. Luke will use the designation "savior" thirty times in his gospel!

PURPOSE: Mary was chosen to be the mother of Jesus because Jesus was to have a purpose—to be our Redeemer.

SUMMARY: We use the term "salvation history" as a shorthand way of talking about the whole mystery of salvation. The final act begins here with Mary, the mother of the Redeemer.

MUSINGS:

1. When Isaiah spoke his prophecy, things in Israel were about as bad as they could get. Yet, as dark as they were, at that moment, Isaiah was inspired to promise once again a "Savior" for Israel. It will not be Hezekiah, the son of King Ahaz. No, it would be Jesus, the son of the Virgin Mary.

2. Midrash: We have used the term before and will meet it again throughout this collection. Luke uses midrash in a special way. First he announces or gives us the revelation about Jesus. Then he calls up Scripture passages that support and confirm the revelation. He does not give us a list of Scripture passages and then conclude with Christ. He begins with Christ. As St. Luke reflected on the Hebrew Scriptures, he saw them through the eyes of Christian faith. Time and time again, he will allude to these promises to show us that Jesus is the one to save us. And Mary was his mother, Mother of the Savior.

3. As suggested in the exegesis of the gospel, the numbers tell the story. Luke uses "fulfilled" eight times. In the whole of his gospel he uses the word "savior" thirty times. It is not a numbers game, however. This observation captures the meaning of our celebration in a very special

way. Jesus is the fulfillment of all the promises. He is indeed the Savior of the world.

4. The whole of the history of salvation, from Adam and Eve in the Garden through Abraham and Sarah to David and his posterity, all is fulfilled in Jesus. He will bring the gifts of justice and peace.

RELATION TO THE EUCHARIST: In the Eucharist we remember the passion, death, and resurrection of Jesus and we remember that it begins here, with Mary, his mother, mother of the Redeemer.

Sources

Guide for the Christian Assembly: A Background Book of the Mass, 9 vols., ed. Thierry Maertens and Jean Frisque (Notre Dame, IN: Fides Publishers, 1971), I:178, 2187.

6. THE BLESSED VIRGIN MARY AND THE EPIPHANY OF THE LORD

Exegesis of the First Reading: Isaiah 60:1-6

The glory of the Lord shines upon you.

The city of Jerusalem was built in such a way that at sunrise, the city walls are brilliant while the valleys below are still in darkness. It is a beautiful sight even today. It is still just as Isaiah described it. It is a shining light to those who walk below in the darkness. Isaiah uses this image of the glory of Jerusalem to show how the Messiah will lighten the whole world.

"Glory" is a word the Scriptures use to tell us something that cannot really be spoken. "Glory" is a sign of the presence of God. It was the "Glory" displayed on Mount Sinai (Exod 16) when the Lord God gave the commandments to Moses. It was the "Glory" in the temple of Solomon (1 Kgs 8:10) at the time of its dedication. When the Scriptures use this term, they are telling us that something sacred, something awful, something wonderful, is taking place.

In this passage Isaiah uses the image of the sun shining on the city to tell us that the Lord is within the city and it is the Lord who gives it its brilliance. Isaiah tells us that the whole world is drawn to Jerusalem because this is where the "Glory" of the Lord resides. People of all nations are invited. It is a universal invitation.

Exegesis of the Gospel Reading: Matthew 2:1-12

Entering the house, they saw the child with Mary, his mother.

Astrology was the science of the time and was important in explaining extraordinary events. Thus, the visit by the magi need not be considered just a legend. People all over the world were expecting great things. Roman oppression was everywhere. All people were waiting for a golden age; they were hoping for a Messiah. In St. Matthew's account we find the first sign of the universal kingdom of Christ. What may be legend is that there were three kings. The number "three" is inferred from the number of gifts that the Scriptures describe and from the significance of their interpretation.

An important lesson we learn is that the Scriptures are best illustrated and understood by the Scriptures. In this passage about King Herod, we can see a parallel to the book of Numbers where Balaam is asked to curse Israel (Num 22:2-4). He refuses. Subsequently Balaam speaks of a star rising in Jacob (Num 24:17). It may be an allusion to King David but the parallel is clear. Herod wishes harm for the newborn child and is thwarted in his attempt by the star that rises in Jacob.

PURPOSE: The revelation of Christ reveals Mary as well.

SUMMARY: Of all the ways artists have pictured Jesus and Mary, perhaps the most frequent portrayal is of the picture described in this gospel passage: Mary showing off her child for all to see.

MUSINGS:

1. Without any desire to be "cute" we have all heard stories about the pride of Jewish mothers in the accomplishment of their children. This feast gives us, if you will, the picture of the Jewish mother par excellence.

2. Mary already knows by the message of an angel that this infant is the Savior. She knows of his wondrous conception and the promises made about him by the angel. She knows that he is the light that has

come into the world. She knows that he is the Savior of the world. She knows that she has been chosen by the Lord to present Jesus to the world. Quite properly, she is proud and happy to show him off.

3. She was the instrument of his birth and now, as she presents him to the magi, she is the instrument of his manifestation, his epiphany. The word "epiphany" means to show off, to manifest, to reveal. This Scripture passage is used on the feast of the Epiphany of the Lord, where Jesus is shown to the world. It shows, as well, the universal character of the coming of the Lord.

4. This was the Lord's first appearance to the Gentiles. It is Mary who presents Jesus to the world, the shepherds, and now the magi. Later, it is she who will present him to Jerusalem. Quite appropriately, therefore, we may celebrate her and the Epiphany of the Lord.

5. Mary is the Mother of God, the Mother of the Savior. She is the instrument that God uses to manifest Jesus to the world.

RELATION TO THE EUCHARIST: Christ was not revealed for his own sake but for ours. To this end he gave us the Eucharist.

Sources

Guide for the Christian Assembly: A Background Book of the Mass, 9 vols., ed. Thierry Maertens and Jean Frisque (Notre Dame, IN: Fides Publishers, 1971), I:252, 254.

7. THE BLESSED VIRGIN MARY AND THE PRESENTATION OF THE LORD

Exegesis of the First Reading: Malachi 3:1-4

The Lord whom you seek will come to his temple.

Malachi was a very radical prophet. For him, the Messiah was to be more than just a messenger from the Lord; he was to be the Lord himself. Malachi was writing after the exile and after the temple of Jerusalem had been rebuilt. Worship in the temple was very important but needed to be pure and offered properly. Both the people and especially the priests always need greater purification to offer this worship.

The word for "messenger" is sometimes translated as "angel." It is through the messenger that the Lord's will is carried out here on the earth. In this case through the eyes of faith, we see Jesus as that "messenger" and much more than a messenger. He is, as the prophet puts it, the Lord himself who "will come to the temple."

Malachi's prophecy gives us a new prism with which to view the Savior. Other prophets saw Jesus, the Messiah, as the son of David. Malachi, however, prophesied that there will be a purified priesthood and a sacrifice that would please the Lord. All the titles that Malachi attributes to the "messenger of the covenant" are fulfilled in Jesus. He is the "refiner's fire," the "fuller's lye," and the priest who will offer the true "sacrifice."

Exegesis of the Gospel Reading: Luke 2:27-35

A sword will pierce your very soul.

The stories of the first two chapters of St. Luke are so familiar that we frequently fail to recognize just how complex and beautiful they are. In this particular passage, he announces the entrance of Jesus into the temple of Jerusalem. Luke then goes out of his way to quote from or allude to reference passages and give parallels to ten different places in the Scriptures.

There was a requirement found in Leviticus 12:2-8 whereby a woman must present her son to the Lord. The law said that the firstborn of every creature belongs to God and was most appropriately applied when Mary presented Jesus in the temple.

The most dramatic illustration of the prophecy of Malachi is found in our first reading where the Messiah comes to the temple in person. The prophet Daniel had spoken with the angel Gabriel and uttered the prophecy of the seventy weeks that are fulfilled in Jesus (Dan 9:24-27). We recall that the ark of the covenant is brought to its rightful place (2 Sam 6). In addition to these references to the book of Leviticus, there are allusions to the law given in Exodus (Exod 13:11; Lev 5:7) and insights reinforced in Genesis 32:31, Deuteronomy 4:33, Isaiah 49:6, Ezra 5:1, and Wisdom 6:22-23.

This is a powerful passage of Scripture.

PURPOSE: While this may not be the beginning of the public mission of Jesus, it is setting the stage.

SUMMARY: All people were waiting for the Messiah who had been promised by God and prophesied in the Scriptures. This feast reminds us that the time is now. What had been anticipated is realized.

MUSINGS:

1. As suggested above, Malachi was a very radical reformer. For him, now that the temple had been rebuilt, there must be a deeper reform and renewal, a change of life. With the rebuilding of the temple, the worship renewed and restored; hearts too must be renewed.

2. We do not go to the temple of Jerusalem to worship but we do go to the new Jerusalem, the church. We are the ones who need to change. All of us need to conform more and more to the holiness that is idealized by the temple and to which Malachi exhorts us.

3. Celebrations of Mary are not simple expressions of our love and devotion to her. They are that, of course, but they are more. We have our celebrations so that we can become more and more like her, refined and polished through suffering.

4. The prophecy of Simeon marks Mary's first sorrow. In our devotions we can trace six more. Her sufferings begin here and continue throughout her life with a climax on Calvary. Calvary is not that far from Bethlehem.

5. Later in the gospel we will find Mary standing beneath the cross of Jesus. We might reflect that he is the one true priest who offers the ultimate sacrifice, the one real sacrifice, and the final sacrifice. Mary is there.

6. Our celebration of Mary is as complex as the gospel reading itself. Our title, "The Blessed Virgin Mary and the Presentation of the Lord," is an invitation to share in her holiness. This is a feast that calls us to conversion of heart.

RELATION TO THE EUCHARIST: As we prepare to celebrate the Eucharist, we might recall the image of Malachi about how we are to be purified, refined like gold and silver, so that we may make due sacrifice to the Lord.

Sources

The Jerome Biblical Commentary, ed. Raymond E. Brown, Joseph A. Fitzmyer, and Roland E. Murphy (Englewood Cliffs, NJ: Prentice-Hall, 1968).

The Collegeville Bible Commentary, ed. Dianne Bergant and Robert J. Karris (Collegeville, MN: Liturgical Press, 1989).

Guide for the Christian Assembly: A Background Book of the Mass, 9 vols., ed. Thierry Maertens and Jean Frisque (Notre Dame, IN: Fides Publishers, 1971), I:170, 233.

8. OUR LADY OF NAZARETH

I

Exegesis of the First Reading: Galatians 4:4-7

God sent his Son, born of a woman, born under the law.

Saint Paul makes three points in this passage. One, the reality of the incarnation: Christ was "born of a woman." Two, he is pointing out the mission of Christ, which is to allow us to be born of the Spirit so that we too might call out "Abba, Father." His third point is that this is a historical event, at a particular moment in time.

Taking this passage from the whole letter to the Galatians is like taking a stone from a mosaic and examining it. The passage itself is beautiful and complex but its real function is to give us a glimpse of the total picture of salvation about which Paul is writing. At that point in history, the way from childhood to adulthood was clearly defined. A child, even if she or he were the primary heir and had already inherited great wealth, had no power of administration. Only when the child became an adult would he or she acquire that power. This is what St. Paul is saying to us. With the coming of Christ we become adult children of God.

Exegesis of the Gospel Reading: Luke 2:22, 39-40

They returned to their own home of Nazareth.
The child grew to maturity, and he was filled with wisdom.

In this gospel selection and in this feast, we commemorate two separate events, the presentation of Jesus in the temple and the hidden home life of Nazareth.

Scholars tell us that the way St. Luke tells the story of Jesus is to tell it twice. He tells it in capsule form in the infancy narratives and he will expand that story in his latter chapters. Another characteristic of Luke's is the importance of the temple in Jerusalem.

Early in Luke's gospel, Mary and Joseph bring Jesus to the temple. There is no mention of his redemption as required in Exodus 13:13. Rather, Jesus belongs in the temple. He belongs to the heavenly Father. This presentation symbolizes what is eternally true. Nothing can separate him from the Father. Mary is the instrument of this act of presentation.

In the second part of the passages, we have a picture of the life of Nazareth. Once again Luke reminds us of the humanity of Jesus. He had a family, a city, a province to which he was connected historically. While we do not know a single detail of that life in Nazareth, we do know all that the Holy Spirit wanted us to know: that Jesus grew and became strong, he was filled with wisdom, and the favor of God was upon him.

It is worth noting that one of the chief differences between the authentic gospels and apocryphal works written about Jesus is the absence of gratuitous miracles. Luke does not "make up" anything just to fill up Jesus' time at Nazareth.

PURPOSE: The time at Nazareth is a time of silence in which to reflect.

SUMMARY: Jesus spent ten times more time with Mary at Nazareth than he spent in his public life with his apostles and disciples.

MUSINGS:

1. Paul is very clear about what Christianity is all about: redemption. It is the work of God to bring about redemption. To accomplish his will, he sent his son "born of a woman."

2. For all our devotion to Mary, St. Paul reminds us that it is by the work of God that we call God our Father. Still, Mary is near.

3. Luke will not let us forget what is important to us. He uses the word "fulfill" at least eight times in the first two chapters of his gospel. Jesus is the fulfillment of all the hopes and dreams of Israel. Luke will use the words "to save" as many as thirty times in his gospel! He reminds us that Nazareth is part of this salvation history even though we know little of what actually happened there.

4. Mary is always an instrument that God uses. Note the phrase "When the days were completed for *their* purification." It was "their" purification, but the purpose of the trip to the temple was to "present him to the Lord."

5. This story is the heart of all the infancy narratives, the heart of the gospel. Jesus is brought to the temple and presented to the Father. The eternal Word of God becomes man, and now, as man, presented to the Father. The wonder of it!

6. From the very beginning Mary is there. Mary is united with Jesus as he fulfills his mission, which is to be our Savior. As she was the instrument of the Father in bringing Jesus to this world, so she is now the instrument God uses to bring Jesus to us. Salvation is the gift to us from God through Mary.

Exegesis of the Alternate Gospel Reading: Luke 2:41-52

Jesus went down with them and came to Nazareth,
where he was subject to them.

To understand the message of this passage of the gospel, we must return to the point we made before about understanding what St. Luke is telling us in the infancy narratives. In his first two chapters, Luke is reflecting the entire story of Jesus in miniature. While Mary and Joseph do not understand, this foreshadows the lack of understanding on the part of the disciples of Jesus. In the same way the loss of "three days" in the temple reflects symbolically the "three days" Jesus will be in the tomb. Jesus is a teacher in the midst of the teachers. Gently but firmly Jesus assumes his proper relationship with the Father. He has a special work, a special mission, which he must carry out both now and in his public life.

His work will involve pain, sorrow, and separation. In the end, however, there will be the joy of the resurrection. We can see this in a special way in the sorrows of Mary. Their separation was the cause of sorrow but their reunion a cause of joy. In the years at Nazareth Mary begins to see something of the complex picture of Jesus.

This journey to Jerusalem foreshadows the final journey to Jerusalem. The journey "to Jerusalem" characterizes Luke's entire gospel.

MUSINGS:

1. Among the many popular devotions to Mary, devotion to her Seven Sorrows is one that has the most solid scriptural foundation. This incident of the loss of Jesus in the temple is the third on the list of Mary's sorrows.

2. We must recall that St. Luke presents the whole message of Jesus in capsule form through the infancy narratives. Here he describes the

separation, the search, the anxiety of Mary and Joseph. In doing so, the question Mary asks shows us the depth of sorrow she experiences at this time. Later, on Calvary, she will experience an even more painful separation and even deeper anxiety.

3. As we celebrate this event with the title of "Our Lady of Nazareth," the Scripture readings suggest that life at Nazareth was much more than an idyllic break in the gospel narrative. Earlier Mary had been told that a sword would pierce her heart. Now we are told that she "kept all these things in her heart." It was a time for reflection. It was a time of waiting. Time was a prerequisite for mission.

4. Could those three days that Jesus was lost symbolize or predict his time in the tomb?

5. Is it here that Jesus begins to know he is different, that he is special, that he is the Son of God?

RELATION TO THE EUCHARIST: Paul reminds us that it was in the fullness of time that "God sent his Son, born of a woman," to be our Savior. Today, this moment offers us a time to realize that fullness in our lives as we are united with Christ and this woman, in the Eucharist.

Sources

Guide for the Christian Assembly: A Background Book of the Mass, 9 vols., ed. Thierry Maertens and Jean Frisque (Notre Dame, IN: Fides Publishers, 1971), I:237, 241.

The Jerome Biblical Commentary, ed. Raymond E. Brown, Joseph A. Fitzmyer, and Roland E. Murphy (Englewood Cliffs, NJ: Prentice-Hall, 1968). (Three days symbolic of Jesus in the tomb.)

William Barclay, The Daily Study Bible Series, rev. ed., New Testament commentary (Louisville, KY: Westminster John Knox, 1975).

II

Exegesis of the First Reading: Colossians 3:12-17

May the fullness of Christ's message live within you.

The official introduction to the entire set of Masses states that some selections were made to illustrate the virtues that have always been associated with Mary. This is one such selection. We do not know what happened in Nazareth for those thirty years. Here, St. Paul gives us a picture of an ideal Christian relationship. With very little imagination we might suggest it reflects life at Nazareth.

This passage reads almost as though it were a poem or a song. Like a poem or a song, it reveals in a lyrical way an important description of what it is to be a follower of Christ. Paul is drawing on his Hebrew background. In the Hebrew Scriptures to be "holy" was to be chosen, to be set apart. Here he is suggesting that we who have been born into Christ have been set apart. Thus chosen, we are now being sent into the world to be an example to the world. By our holiness we will attract others to Christ. The followers of Christ must be an example to the world that there is a better way. Paul describes the character of one so united to Christ. He or she is a person of heartfelt compassion, kindness, humility, gentleness, and patience.

Exegesis of the Gospel Reading: Matthew 2:13-15, 19-23

He went and lived in a town called Nazareth.

The special key to understanding Matthew's gospel is to realize that he is writing to Jewish Christians and tries to show them that Jesus is the new Moses. We need to recall the Hebrew Scriptures and especially the book of Exodus. There we hear the story of how God "called" Israel from Egypt. Now God will call Jesus from Egypt. Matthew is reminding us of the Passover. In the verses, which are omitted from this selection, there is an account of the massacre of the innocents. Therefore, as Moses had escaped the massacre of the Pharaoh, so now Jesus escapes the massacre of Herod. This promise to deliver the people from Egypt was made to Abraham even before it was made to Moses. The Lord had promised to make Israel a great nation.

The Jewish way of telling stories is called "midrash." It was the way the rabbis understood the Scriptures. Jewish Christians, however, used a slightly different method. Matthew here, and Luke in his gospel, begins with a fact of revelation about Jesus and then recalls Scripture passages that illustrate and/or expand on the revelation itself. The gospel story is not history or biography. It is revelation. It is God's message to his people. God tells us, through the gospel, what God wants us to know.

PURPOSE: While there is very little action at Nazareth, we cannot ignore a major part of the life of Jesus and Mary.

SUMMARY: While we do not make up stories of the life of Jesus, still we are able, from the pictures that the Scriptures give us of Christian life, to project something of the life in Nazareth.

MUSINGS:

1. When St. Paul describes Christian behavior, does he use Jesus and Mary as his models? Does it matter?

2. When St. Paul suggests that the very first characteristic of the Christian is "heartfelt compassion," who other than Mary could he have had in mind?

3. Forgiveness, "the bond of perfection": these virtues filled those silent years at Nazareth.

4. "[D]o everything in the name of the Lord Jesus" sounds very much like Mary at Cana.

5. Today the lives of the saints are the result of exhaustive historical and scholarly research. They provide us with dates and times and circumstances that firmly set the individual saints in their eras. Authors are hired to write biographies. Lists of their virtues are generated by computer. We have gotten used to this modern notion of history.

6. We may speculate on Jesus and Mary from what we know of the characters of the gospels. They were Jews, devout Jews. They lived lives that we see reflected later in their public lives. They were God's chosen ones. Their lives reflected that.

7. Thus when St. Paul speaks of being at peace because of the union "in one body," we are able to see a special allusion to the union of Jesus and Mary.

RELATION TO THE EUCHARIST: Paul reminds us that it was in the fullness of time that "God sent his Son, born of a woman," to be our Savior. Today, this moment offers us a time to realize that fullness in our lives as we are united with Christ and this woman, in the Eucharist.

Sources

Guide for the Christian Assembly: A Background Book of the Mass, 9 vols., ed. Thierry Maertens and Jean Frisque (Notre Dame, IN: Fides Publishers, 1971), I:204, 231.

9. OUR LADY OF CANA

Exegesis of the First Reading: Exodus 19:3-8a

Whatever the Lord has spoken, we will do.

The principle and beautiful image of the book of Exodus here may not be too familiar to city people. At the right time an adult eagle will nudge its chick out of its high standing nest and then as it falls the parent swiftly flies beneath the falling chick to catch it on its own wings. The Lord God uses this image to illustrate his concern and care for his people.

The Lord goes on to describe just how special this people really is. The Lord God speaks directly to the people. It is a very personal relationship and it is here that we find the words that the prophets in later generations will use to call the people back to the right path as a kingdom of priests, as a holy nation.

Prominent in this passage is the response of the people. The covenant will not be forced on the people. After Moses had reminded them of the privileges that the Lord had conferred upon them, the people agreed as they answered freely, "Everything the LORD has said, we will do."

This short passage is at the very heart of the Exodus story. The book outlines the love and care of the Lord for his people and their willing response. This invitation of the Lord and the response of the people will be like a musical fugue throughout all the Scriptures.

Exegesis of the Gospel Reading: John 2:1-11

Do whatever he tells you.

Saint John has a master plan for his whole gospel and therefore there are no insignificant details. As we look at each passage, we must always see it in relation to his master plan.

As John records the "days" in chapters 1 and 2 of his gospel, we find that this incident at Cana is on the seventh day. John is recounting for us the seven days of the new creation. This incident, this work, the marriage at Cana performed on the seventh day has its special significance.

With this in mind, we must note that the failure of the wine was much more than an embarrassing catering fault. In the first creation in the book of Genesis, there was the woman Eve whose actions are described as initiating the "fall." Now at the initiative of Mary, we have the beginning of the new creation. The words she uses when she instructs the waiters echo the words in Exodus to do whatever Jesus asks of them.

This chapter and chapter 19 are intimately related. First there is the word "woman," which Jesus uses to address his mother. He will use the same word to address her from the cross. There is the word "hour." At Cana it has not yet come, but Calvary is the hour.

John lists this as the "first" of the signs that Jesus will give to us. Here too he mentions the first response to Jesus' signs, the belief of his disciples.

This passage from the Gospel of John is so important that it will be used eight more times in the Collection of Masses of the Blessed Virgin Mary. Each time we reflect on it, we will see more deeply into its meaning.

PURPOSE: The incident at Cana initiates the new creation.

SUMMARY: The day, the hour, the name, the new wine: this passage with its reference to the passion and death of the Lord is critical to the whole New Testament story.

MUSINGS:

1. The passage from John's gospel is frequently used at weddings and reflects the desire of the couple to have Jesus and Mary grace the beginnings of their marriage. A great idea, but thinking of it only in this way misses much of the deeper mystery of the gospel.

2. This passage marks the beginning of the public ministry of Jesus. It also indicates in a striking way the powerful intercession of Mary, which prompts Jesus to anticipate his "hour."

3. The Scriptures of both the Hebrew and Christian covenants are a single body of revelation. What is said in the Old Testament through signs and symbol is experienced in the New Testament in the unfolding of the divine plan. At the outset of the public ministry of Jesus, we have Mary using the words taken from Exodus where the people assented to the covenant and pledged themselves to the Lord. There is more here than extra fine wine.

4. Our reflections take us beyond that of the graciousness and intercessory power of Mary. They illuminate the bond that binds Mary to her son in the unfolding of the divine plan. We may consider the change of water into wine as the way Jesus uses to remind us of the great transformation of wine into his sacred blood.

5. Cana, like every other episode in the gospels, is part of the whole revelation. It invites us to "Do whatever the Lord says."

6. This whole feast reminds us that we too are borne up on eagle wings; we too are that special possession of the Lord, a kingdom of priests, a holy nation, and a people set apart.

RELATION TO THE EUCHARIST: The gospel passage gives us the day, Mary gives us the command, and Jesus himself refers to his hour. As we celebrate the Eucharist, we join Jesus and Mary at that hour.

Sources

Guide for the Christian Assembly: A Background Book of the Mass, 9 vols., ed. Thierry Maertens and Jean Frisque (Notre Dame, IN: Fides Publishers, 1971), VI:200.

Marian Reflections: The Angelus Messages of Pope John Paul II, ed. David O. Brown (Washington, NJ: AMI Press, 1990), 30.

Do Whatever He Tells You: Reflections and Proposals for Promoting Marian Devotion (Rome: General Curia OSM, 1983), 47.

Guide for the Christian Assembly, II:34.

Marian Reflections, 35.

Do Whatever He Tells You, 47, 76.

Servants of the *Magnificat*: The Canticle of the Blessed Virgin and Consecrated Life (Rome: General Curia OSM, 1996), 15, 20, 39, 92, 93.

John 2:1-11: Francis Moloney, *The Gospel of John*, ed. Daniel J. Harrington, Sacra Pagina Series (Collegeville, MN: Liturgical Press, 1998), 63.

LENTEN SEASON

The Masses of this collection for the Lenten season have Mary as a Mother of Sorrows as the principle characteristic.

10. HOLY MARY, DISCIPLE OF THE LORD

Exegesis of the First Reading: Sirach 51:13-18, 20-22

My heart delighted in wisdom.

If at the time they had the designations of conservative and liberal, Sirach would be a strong conservative. The Greeks had conquered Palestine, and Greek influence was changing the language and the culture of the nation. Should the people go along to get along? No, says Sirach. The book of Sirach was written about the year 180 BC. His intention was to support and preserve the Jewish religious traditions. While the Greeks promise happiness, Sirach contends that the only guarantee of happiness will be found in wisdom, which he calls "she." He reminds his readers that true wisdom is from above, from God, not from humans. The search for God requires a moral conversion, clean hands, and fidelity to the traditions. One must not be silent about the discovery of wisdom. When we have found her, we must be faithful to her and we must praise her.

Exegesis of the Gospel Reading: Luke 2:41-52

The mother of Jesus treasured all these things in her heart.

This is one of the most interesting, important, and complex passages in Luke's gospel. Whenever we look at any passage in Luke's gospel, we must reflect on the structure he gives to all his stories. Consistently, in these first two chapters, St. Luke will tell us beforehand, in sign, symbol, and narrative, what he will tell us again later and more directly in the life of Jesus. In this passage, the separation, the anxiety, the loss for "three days," as well as the joy and the mystery surrounding the reunion, all point to the future, to the similar separation, anxiety, and finally joy at the death and resurrection of Jesus.

When Mary says, "Your father and I," Jesus gently but definitively transfers the title "father" from St. Joseph to his heavenly Father. Some commentators suggest that it was at this time that Jesus himself became aware of who he was, the unique Son of God.

While the official public ministry of Jesus will not begin for another eighteen years or so, yet this first of his public acts is set in the temple of Jerusalem. This would not have been their first trip to the temple. They made the trip each year. Why did he show himself this year? This is typical of Luke's gospel. The last act of his public life before the Last Supper, the crucifixion, and resurrection will likewise be in the temple when he drives out the money changers.

Exegesis of the Alternate Gospel Reading: Matthew 12:46-50

Extending his hands toward the disciples, he said:
Here are my mother and my brothers.

Chapter 12 of Matthew's gospel is pivotal. The chapter consists of a series of controversies about what Jesus is teaching and how he agrees or diverges from the law as the scribes and Pharisees were interpreting it. The entire exchange clarifies our understanding of the teaching of Jesus.

At this time, Mary and his brothers wished to see him. When we look at John 7:5 and Mark 3:21, we get the impression the family of Jesus never seemed to understand him. For his part, his remarks about them seem sharp. They are not any sharper than the conditions he had earlier set down for those he had called to be his disciples. Now he is calling his family to join him as disciples. What he is revealing to them and to us is that it is neither status nor kinship that makes us disciples but intimacy.

PURPOSE: Saint Augustine said that Mary is more blessed because of her faith than because of her motherhood.

SUMMARY: Again we have the expression that she kept these things in her heart. What things? The events, the words, the teachings of Jesus.

As she grew in faith and discipleship she became more and more an example for us.

MUSINGS:

1. This celebration is about accepting the word of God. Sirach, the sage, tells us that true wisdom is from God. Where else would Mary, young and innocent, find that word? She had already, with tongue and lips, given grateful praise to the Lord. Later that "word" would come to her.

2. When Mary sees Jesus in the temple, in the midst of the teachers, she sees and hears him in a new way. She knows him as the true wisdom of the Lord. When she hears it in the words of Jesus, so removing the name "father" from Joseph and giving it to his heavenly "Father," she has a new insight into who her son is.

3. Mary knows what it is to lose Jesus. She knows that she had to search to find him. "Finding Jesus" makes her a disciple of the Lord. The three days and three nights were not wasted. She taught us what it is to search.

4. As Mary observed Jesus grow in wisdom, age, and favor before God and neighbors, she too continued to grow in the knowledge of what it is to be his disciple.

5. Commentators have observed that in the majority of the world's religions there is an affinity based on kinship or nationality. Even today, the descendants of Aaron received a special reverence from the Jewish community. The direct descendants of Muhammad have a special place in Islam. Not so with Christianity.

6. The scene shown in Matthew's gospel is found, with different nuances, in the gospels of Mark (3:21) and John (7:5). There can be no doubt about the message: to be a disciple of the Lord requires faith, not kinship.

7. If we reflect on these passages, we find that Jesus does not reject his family and his kin. Rather, he reveals to them, and to us, that there is something more important than kinship in his kingdom.

8. In our devotion to Mary, the fact that she is the mother of Jesus is the source of all her special graces and privileges. As the *Theotokos*, she is the Mother of God. This is the foundation of the titles commemorated in this entire set of Masses of the Blessed Virgin. The words of Jesus, however, remind us that as important as that privilege might be, it was more important that she is also a disciple.

RELATION TO THE EUCHARIST: Luke has a way of introducing us to the passion, death, and resurrection of Jesus well beforehand. So as we read and ponder the words of this gospel story, we are preparing ourselves to celebrate that passion, death, and resurrection.

Sources

Sirach: *Guide for the Christian Assembly: A Background Book of the Mass*, 9 vols., ed. Thierry Maertens and Jean Frisque (Notre Dame, IN: Fides Publishers, 1971), II:375.
Luke: Ibid., II:209.
Matthew: Ibid., VI:195.

11. THE BLESSED VIRGIN MARY AT THE FOOT OF THE CROSS

I

Exegesis of the First Reading: Romans 8:31b-39

God did not spare his own Son.

The essential theme of St. Paul's letter to the Romans is hope. In the eighth chapter of his letter, we have a hymn in honor of the love God has for us. God's love is the root cause of our hope. Paul imagines himself, and us along with him, before a bar of justice. Like Job, we are being tested. He asks who can possibly accuse us of anything. We are, after all, God's chosen ones. Who or what can possibly separate us from this love of God by which Christ has redeemed us? Not anguish, not distress, not peril, not the sword. Nothing can separate us. He ends with a beautiful personal testimony of the strength of the union between himself and the love of God in Christ Jesus.

Exegesis of the Gospel Reading: John 19:25-27

There by the cross of Jesus stood his mother.

This Scripture passage from John's gospel is used nine times in this collection and specifically in the next three formulae of this section. Its frequent use underlines its importance, complexity, and nuances. Full treatment of this passage is covered in the three Mass formulae.

We have been taught that the first and best rule for interpreting the Scriptures is to be found in the Scriptures themselves. When the gospel passage reflects a portion of another book of the Scriptures or when it reflects on something that had already been said in the same gospel, that passage takes on a special significance.

Also when dealing with the gospels, nothing is accidental. God reveals to us as much as God wants us to know and understand. Human authors are the instruments of God and, as such, these human instruments may put their own imprint on the stories they tell. This is why each gospel is different yet all comes from God.

To understand this passage properly, we must refer to the story of the marriage feast at Cana (Mass no. 9) in chapter 2 of John's gospel. At that time we noted how Mary gently reminds Jesus that there is no wine. Jesus responds with a question and a statement: "Woman, how does your concern affect me? / My hour has not yet come" (John 2:4). Note the address "Woman," and the "hour."

Finally at the conclusion of the account of the wedding feast, St. John tells us that Jesus "revealed his glory, / and his disciples began to believe in him" (2:11).

As we reflect on the story of Cana, we see that much more was going on than a good son indulging his caring mother; there is more here than the family relationship of son and mother. This was an integral part of the gospel story played out on multiple layers.

Now as we come back to our passage in chapter 19 of John, we are at Calvary and the "hour" has come. Once again Jesus addresses Mary as "Woman."

Mary was integral to the story by which his disciples first believed in him at Cana. Now she is integral to the story of salvation that the disciples will take to the world.

PURPOSE: To offer more substance to the stark silhouette of Calvary.

SUMMARY: Every time a child is baptized, every time we make the sign of the cross, our attention is focused on Calvary and the cross of Christ with his Mother standing there.

MUSINGS:

1. The interpretation of a Scripture text in the first millennium will be different from the interpretation of the text in the third millennium. The context is different. So too when we read this passage from the letter to the Romans on the feast of Mary at the Foot of the Cross, it delivers a message that is differently nuanced from when we use it in the thirteenth week of Ordinary Time. When St. Paul asks us today, "Who will separate us from the love of Christ?" his answer takes on a greater depth and poignancy.

2. In chapter 8 of his letter, Paul focuses on the process of justification. In this passage, he lays out the work of the whole Trinity in the process of justification. The love of the Father makes all of us his children. The Spirit takes possession of us to help us grow in this relationship. Finally, the Son comes to earth as the way in which our relationship to God is consummated. It is a way of pain, hardship, suffering, death, and finally resurrection. It was the path for Jesus. It is the path for us.

3. As we listen to the word spoken by Paul in the first reading, we too may ask, "If God is for us, who can be against us?" If God "did not spare his own Son . . . [w]ho will bring a charge against [us]?" Yes, Christ died, but he was raised to life again. He is the source of our hope.

4. As we look to Mary, at the foot of the cross, the words of Paul are almost like lyrics of a song he sings to us or the colors of a picture he paints for us. Who will separate her from the love of Christ: anguish, distress, persecution, peril, or the sword?

5. The sword! In a special way, the sword! These words apply to Mary. Neither death nor life! As we listen to the last two verses of this passage from Paul, could he have been thinking of Mary? Of whom but Mary can he be thinking? "For I am convinced that neither death, nor life, / nor angels, nor principalities, / nor present things, nor future things, nor powers, nor height, nor depth, / nor any other creature will be able to separate us / from the love of God in Christ Jesus."

6. As Mary was integral to the story by which his disciples first believed in Jesus at Cana, so now she is integral to the story of salvation that the disciples will take to the world. The next time we see Mary, she will be in the midst of the disciples. "All these devoted themselves with one accord to prayer, together with some women, and Mary the mother of Jesus, and his brothers" (Acts 1:14).

7. Too often we find that devotion to Mary at the foot of the cross is summed up in the Pietà. The tender, sad picture of Mary and her dead

Son that moves us to pity is so vivid that it is impressed on our minds and expressed in our devotions. The picture is moving, lovely, important. It has drawn many to a deeper love of Jesus and Mary. Those who have suffered the loss of a loved one, especially a son, share deeply with Mary and know that Mary shares deeply with them. It is more than piety, however, that makes this scene so important in our devotional life. Its roots go deeply into the center of our faith.

8. Mary at the foot of the cross draws our attention to more than her sorrows. She draws us to the central mystery of our faith—the love of God in Christ Jesus. On Calvary, Jesus gave Mary to the church and to the world.

9. We would never know Mary's name if all we read was John's gospel. In this gospel she is always "the mother of Jesus" or when Jesus himself addresses her, at Cana and here on Calvary, she is "Woman."

10. Neither does Jesus give us a name for the disciple whom he loved who was standing there. He is much more than just an individual. No doubt there is the concern of a son for his mother in the coming days. It is indeed an act of filial piety. But much more was happening. Can the unnamed disciple be me?

RELATION TO THE EUCHARIST: What better preparation can we have for the celebration of the memorial of Christ's passion than a reflection on the way his mother Mary celebrated that first passion?

Sources

Romans: *Guide for the Christian Assembly: A Background Book of the Mass*, 9 vols., ed. Thierry Maertens and Jean Frisque (Notre Dame, IN: Fides Publishers, 1971), VIII:220.
John: Ibid., III:298.
New American Bible, Revised Edition, note for John 19:26-27.

12. THE BLESSED VIRGIN MARY AT THE FOOT OF THE CROSS

II

Exegesis of the First Reading: Judith 13:17-20

You have averted our ruin before our God.

The story of Judith is not necessarily a historical account. Rather it is a story set in the context of the exile to show the people of Israel that in spite of the difficult times, God is still with them. In the structure of the story we can detect a reflection of the exodus story. A hostile army was about to destroy the Jews. Judith used her talents to deceive the evil king, to get near him and then to destroy him. The nation was delivered. The times and circumstances are very different, but in the end the Lord's intervention leads to victory. This time, the woman Judith, through her faith and prayer, is the instrument of victory.

The church regards all the Scriptures as a single body. What is found in one place clarifies what is said in another. The Jewish people were suffering the privations of an exile and were tempted to discouragement. Israel can be saved only when the individual subordinates personal needs to the common good. What was important was her fidelity in spite of all the odds.

Exegesis of the Gospel Reading: John 19:25-27

There by the cross of Jesus stood his mother.

When the word "mother" is used five times in these verses, its use certainly emphasizes the importance of Mary's place on Calvary and a clue to her function. On the other hand, when John does not use Mary's name, that too is important, for her function is more important than her person.

When Jesus chooses to speak to Mary, it is significant. She was the first person to believe his word. We can believe, therefore, that when Jesus commends his mother to St. John, it is more than an act of simple filial piety. When John in turn takes her to his own home, he is providing more than shelter. It is the initiation of the new family of Jesus. She assumes the maternal role of the "Mother" in the new family of Jesus that is established on the cross.

At the conclusion of the account of the wedding feast at Cana, John tells us that "Jesus revealed his glory, / and his disciples began to believe in him" (2:11).

It is the hour of his glory, yet he is abandoned by all his disciples except for Mary, the beloved disciple, and three other women.

There seems to be four women present with the beloved disciple John. Scholars read the gospels but can only conjecture who they were.

PURPOSE: Mary on Calvary stands before us all at the foot of the cross.

SUMMARY: What happened on Calvary? We all know, yet each time we look at this picture we learn of new depths. We see in Mary the courage and resolve of Judith and we rejoice in her victory.

MUSINGS:

1. The story of Judith attempts to make clear that all the virtues praised in the Scriptures flourish in Mary, the first and most perfect disciple of Christ.

2. This same passage from the book of Judith is used also in the celebration in honor of The Immaculate Heart of the Blessed Virgin Mary (no. 28), The Blessed Virgin Mary, Pillar of Faith (no. 35), and Our Lady of Ransom (no. 43). Each feast attempts to portray Mary's strength, fortitude, and virtue. On the feast of Our Lady of Sorrows, we are drawn to her fidelity. She was with Jesus until the end.

3. There were four women and one man at the cross of Jesus on Calvary. The feminist movement has performed an important service to our society, male and female. It made us aware. Not all injustices have been righted or evils eliminated, but with the growing awareness came a chance to reflect again, with new insights, into how God used the instrumentality of women in working out the salvation of all God's people.

4. The Lord God chose even the powerless of this world to confound the strong. He chose Judith, an exile, a foreigner, a woman, to work his will against the invading king. She prevailed and the people blessed her for it. They blessed her with words that seem to anticipate the blessings given by the angel to Mary, the mother of Jesus.

5. Mary, standing at the foot of the cross on Calvary, has a rightful place in the mystery of salvation. The words applied to Judith deserve

to apply to Mary: "Your deed of hope will never be forgotten" (13:19). The image, the scene, the reality gives us a vivid picture of a heroic woman whose deeds will never be forgotten.

RELATION TO THE EUCHARIST: We celebrate in signs and symbol a very real event. Our recollection of the most real event of Calvary prepares us to celebrate with signs the reality of our salvation.

Sources

Judith: *The Jerome Biblical Commentary*, ed. Raymond E. Brown, Joseph A. Fitzmyer, and Roland E. Murphy (Englewood Cliffs, NJ: Prentice-Hall, 1968), 25.

Judith: *The Collegeville Bible Commentary*, ed. Dianne Bergant and Robert J. Karris (Collegeville, MN: Liturgical Press, 1989).

John: *Guide for the Christian Assembly: A Background Book of the Mass*, 9 vols., ed. Thierry Maertens and Jean Frisque (Notre Dame, IN: Fides Publishers, 1971), III:198.

Francis Moloney, *The Gospel of John*, ed. Daniel J. Harrington, Sacra Pagina Series (Collegeville, MN: Liturgical Press, 1998), 501.

13. THE COMMENDING OF THE BLESSED VIRGIN MARY

Exegesis of the First Reading: 2 Maccabees 7:1, 20-29

Because of her hope in the Lord,
this admirable mother bore their deaths with honor.

The message of the book of Maccabees is that God continues to watch over his people even when tragedy strikes and all seems lost. The author of the book of Maccabees, written about 125 BC, drew inspiration from the prophet Jeremiah (15:9), where the prophet developed one of his prophecies using the example of a woman with seven sons as a sign of God's abundant blessings. He goes on to say that even with such blessings, this woman would "swoon" in the face of the sins of the people of Jerusalem.

In the second book of Maccabees the author builds on that image. He wants to strengthen the Jewish people. They were under siege at the time. They must take courage. They must not swoon away. They are to keep the faith. This tragic story tries to show them how to be faithful. They must have utter dependence on God.

When the courageous mother of the Maccabees mentions that the Lord will restore both breath and life to her son, she is probably speaking of her hope for the restoration of Zion. The full revelation of life after death will come with Jesus. Her point is still valid. One must know how to give one's life away to be able to believe that it will be returned.

Exegesis of the Gospel Reading: John 19:25-27

Woman, this is your son.

At Cana St. John set the scene that gave us, as it were, a preview of how our salvation and redemption would be effected. Mary, along with the disciples, believed Jesus, yet at Cana his hour had not yet come. Now on Calvary, his hour has come. It is "the hour" of salvation. Jesus chooses this hour to give, to "commend" his mother to the disciple whom he loves.

Throughout his gospel, John develops a theme of gathering, uniting, bringing together into one. Jesus spoke of gathering other sheep into one fold. Even Caiaphas spoke of one man to die for the sake of many. The chief priest spoke of the many who were coming to believe in Jesus after he had raised Lazarus from the dead. In a word, the mission of Jesus was to establish a community of believers. When this theme is added to the light we received from Cana, then this mutual "commending" of Mary and the disciple, Jesus is truly founding a new family of faith. This passage affirms the maternal role of the mother of Jesus in the mystery of salvation and establishing of this new family of Jesus from the cross.

The whole event is of tremendous significance in the unfolding of the new creation. When Jesus gives his mother to the care of the beloved disciple and then gives the beloved disciple to her, we see the very beginning of the bond of love that has shown itself in all ages expressed in the devotion of Christian people to Mary, the Mother, the Woman.

PURPOSE: Mary becomes the mother of us all.

SUMMARY: At Christmas we celebrate the fact that Mary is the Mother of the Lord. Here on Calvary we celebrate that Mary is made mother of us all through a cross annunciation spoken by Jesus himself.

MUSINGS:

1. In the Scripture passage that the first reading is taken from, the words "womanly reason with manly emotion" may not pass the politically correct speech test (2 Macc 7:21, NABRE). It is simply a metaphor and it is the author's attempt to describe in words taken from his own culture the measure of virtue expected of the faithful. Therefore, the Lectionary for the Marian Masses combines this gendered terminology into one word: "courage."

2. Both readings of this Mass formula present a double bond of family and faith, of pain and suffering, of reality and revelation. The Lord God needs to use words and images to communicate his message to us. We need words, signs, and images to be able to look beyond the surface and get to the realities.

3. Both scenes from Maccabees and Calvary present us with vivid, riveting pictures. The words spoken are no less striking. For the mother of the Maccabees, the words recalled the message of faith received from Moses and the prophets. Her words reflect the blessing given to Israel. She uses words as an exhortation to fidelity. Look to the heavens. Do not be afraid.

4. We must call attention to the fact that it is here (2 Macc 7:28) that we have the first mention of creation from nothing.

5. On Calvary we have a compelling picture to bring us to the hour of salvation. The words of the Son to his mother are likewise compelling. When Jesus uses the word "woman" here on Calvary, he is reflecting the word he used at Cana (John 19:26). When Jesus speaks from the cross, his words reveal a mystery, a new creation, a new family of faith. With his words, the bonds of human relationships are replaced with the bonds of faith. The new Christian family is formed in faith and love.

6. Dare we consider this "commending" of Mary as a Christian Mother's Day?

7. This scene prompted the fathers of Vatican II to say,

> In the public life of Jesus, Mary appears prominently; at the very beginning when at the marriage feast of Cana, moved with pity, she brought about by her intercession the beginning of miracles of Jesus the Messiah (see Jn 2:1-11). In the course of her Son's preaching she accepted the words whereby, in extolling a kingdom beyond the concerns and ties of flesh and blood, he declared blessed those who heard and kept the word of God

(see Mk 3:35; Lk 11:27-28) as she was faithfully doing (see Lk 2:19; 51). Thus the blessed Virgin advanced in her pilgrimage of faith, and faithfully persevered in her union with her Son until she stood at the cross, in keeping with the divine plan (see Jn 19:25), suffering deeply with her only begotten Son, associating herself with his sacrifice in her mother's heart, and lovingly consenting to the immolation of this victim who was born of her. Finally, she was given by the same Christ Jesus dying on the cross as a mother to his disciple, with these words: "Woman, this is your Son" (Jn 19:26-27). (*Lumen Gentium* 58)

RELATION TO THE EUCHARIST: It is just a very short journey from Calvary to the altar, from reflection on the event to the celebration in signs and symbols. Our memory makes both events real.

Sources

Maccabees: *Guide for the Christian Assembly: A Background Book of the Mass*, 9 vols., ed. Thierry Maertens and Jean Frisque (Notre Dame, IN: Fides Publishers, 1971), VII:250.

The Jerome Biblical Commentary, ed. Raymond E. Brown, Joseph A. Fitzmyer, and Roland E. Murphy (Englewood Cliffs, NJ: Prentice-Hall, 1968). (The first biblical mention of creation *ex nihilo*; see also Heb 11.)

2 Macc 7:28: Ibid.

John: Francis Moloney, *The Gospel of John*, ed. Daniel J. Harrington, Sacra Pagina Series (Collegeville, MN: Liturgical Press, 1998), 501ff.

14. THE BLESSED VIRGIN MARY, MOTHER OF RECONCILIATION

Exegesis of the First Reading: 2 Corinthians 5:17-21

On behalf of Christ we implore you to be reconciled to God.

In this passage St. Paul sets out dramatically the transformation effected by Christ. As he sees it, this is the point where the old order ends and the new begins on Calvary. On Calvary God reconciled the whole world to himself through Christ. Calvary is the Christian creation story. In the Hebrew creation story Adam and Eve had sinned and their sin brought alienation and separation from God. Now Paul can speak vividly about new birth by reconciliation because of his own personal experience. Once he persecuted Christ. Then he experienced in himself the change effected by the passion, death, and resurrection of Christ. He knows how radically he has been changed. Now he knows that he has been established as an ambassador of this same reconciliation. He is anxious that all come to know this risen Christ and experience a like reconciliation.

Just before this particular passage, Paul told of how it was the love of God in Christ that impelled him in his ministry. His personal experience of newness of life in Christ is the foundation of his zeal.

Exegesis of the Gospel Reading: John 19:25-27

This is your son. This is your mother.

As we begin to study the Scriptures, one of the first surprises is to find that they were written backward. That is, the account of the passion, death, and resurrection of Jesus was the original focal point of the original story. His death, therefore, is both the high point and the beginning of the gospel. Details of his life and ministry were added later.

When, therefore, St. John tells us that the mother of Jesus was there, that the disciple whom Jesus loved was there, that several women who had been among the first of his followers were there as well, we know that John is telling us something very important. What is he telling us? What do we see? What does it mean? The answers are real even if they are not always evident. There is always a hint of mystery when he tells us any story. There is more than meets the eye.

We would expect that Mary, the mother of Jesus, would be present on Calvary. Jesus may have been rejected, hated, and now crucified, but she is his mother and she is faithful. For his part, Jesus would continue to have filial concerns for his mother. Even as he was setting the foundations for a new creation (see the first reading), he would not neglect his obligations. Still, there was more than filial piety at work.

John's gospel uses the word "hour" at least seventeen times after the time he spoke it to his mother at Cana. He uses the term "hour" to bracket the whole public life of Jesus. And Mary is present on both occasions.

In this short passage, John uses the word "mother" five times. We see Jesus establish a new family from the cross. We see also that there is a special role for Mary. We have a complete reversal of the situation of the prologue (John 1:11), where Jesus came to his own and they did not receive him. Now the disciple, at the command of Jesus, takes her into his own home. We have an unconditional acceptance of his word and unconditional reconciliation.

Purpose: Christ alone has reconciled us to himself, but Mary was there.

Summary: The central mystery of redemption was accomplished on Calvary. The gift of Mary to the disciple John and the gift to John of a mother typify the total reconciliation of humankind with God.

MUSINGS:

1. There are two creation stories in the book of Genesis, one in chapter 1 and the other in chapter 2. Each of those stories, in its own way, paints a vivid, exciting, interesting, captivating picture. Included in the story of creation, there is the story of the fall. The purpose of these two stories is to remind people where they came from and what had happened to them. The stories of creation also serve to remind people of whose garden we now inhabit and our need to care for the earth. Yet they are not the Christian stories of creation.

2. The real "creation story" for Christians begins on Calvary. This is what St. Paul is telling us in the first reading of this celebration. More important than the sun and moon and stars is Jesus. The old things have passed away. If not in reality, at least in importance. We are in a new creation. This is the fundamental understanding of reconciliation: to be reunited with God.

3. Serious theological studies are underway to amplify this notion of the "new creation." As scholars continue their work and in whatever they discover, they will find as well that Mary was near the centerpiece as the new creation was established.

4. Just what is reconciliation? Through the divine mercy because of the obedience of Jesus (Rom 5:10), guilt has been wiped away; this is what theologians call the objective redemption. This is the work of the Lord Jesus alone. Yet Mary was there at the foot of the cross as Jesus accomplished this reconciliation.

5. In the work of the new creation, Mary has a pivotal part. As far back as the third century, Tertullian, one of the early church fathers, put it this way: "Consequently, the Virgin Mary is found obedient, saying 'Behold your handmaid, Lord. Lord, let it be done to me according to your word.' But Eve was disobedient; though still a virgin she did not obey. For as she, though wedded to Adam, was still a virgin . . . being disobedient, she became a cause of death to herself and to all [human] kind. So Mary, having a predestined husband, but none the less a virgin, was obedient and became to herself and to the whole human race a cause of salvation" (*Adv. Haer.* XXII, 4, quoted in *New Dictionary of Theology*). We do not say today that she was the "cause" of redemption but we can never deny that she had her part.

RELATION TO THE EUCHARIST: Reflection on the mystery of love accomplished on Calvary is the best preparation for participation in the mystery of love accomplished by word and sign on the altar.

Sources

Corinthians: *Guide for the Christian Assembly: A Background Book of the Mass*, 9 vols., ed. Thierry Maertens and Jean Frisque (Notre Dame, IN: Fides Publishers, 1971), III:169.

The Jerome Biblical Commentary, ed. Raymond E. Brown, Joseph A. Fitzmyer, and Roland E. Murphy (Englewood Cliffs, NJ: Prentice-Hall, 1968).

Michael O'Carroll, "Mary, Mother of God," in *The New Dictionary of Theology*, ed. J. A. Komonchak, M. Collins, and D. Lane (Collegeville, MN: Liturgical Press, 2000).

Francis Moloney, *The Gospel of John*, ed. Daniel J. Harrington, Sacra Pagina Series (Collegeville, MN: Liturgical Press, 1998), 501ff.

EASTER SEASON

Who was ever better able to celebrate the joy of Easter than Mary? No one was more closely allied with Jesus in his sorrow and therefore no one could be more closely allied than Mary in the joy of his triumph.

15. THE BLESSED VIRGIN MARY AND THE RESURRECTION OF THE LORD

Exegesis of the First Reading: Revelation 21:1-5a

I saw the new Jerusalem, as beautiful as a bride all dressed for her husband.

The book of Revelation is complex and mysterious. It is filled throughout with images, illustrations, and allusions to mysteries that are often difficult to fathom. Commentators, however, are in agreement that this present passage is the high point of the book of Revelation. The last words of this passage, "I make all things new," are the only words spoken directly by the Lord in the whole book.

In this passage we have images of a new creation, the sea, the holy city Jerusalem, a bride, a dwelling place (literally, a tent as in the desert), and an end to all suffering. Each image refers to or reflects a passage or an image from another part of Scripture. Are they images of the church or Mary? Each image is to help us understand who Christ is and what Easter is all about. It is a new creation. The terrors of the sea were removed by the waters of baptism. Jerusalem was for the Jews the focal point of worship but now we have a new Jerusalem. The beauty and delight that a new bride brings to her husband is the kind of beauty and delight we are to experience in the mystery of the resurrection.

"Behold, God's dwelling is with the human race" reflects the presence of God among his people in the garden with Adam and Eve, in the desert through the forty years, and especially in the temple of Jerusalem. Christ, now more than ever, we have an even more intimate "presence" among us with Mary and in the sacraments and the church.

The point of the passage is that all these blessings that had been given to Jerusalem are now conferred on the new people of God as well. The use of this passage in the context of the resurrection and Mary allows us to see that much more is pictured here than we could have imagined. As the word would be applied to the people of God, it may also be applied to Mary, the mother of Jesus. She is there to help wipe away every tear.

Exegesis of the Gospel Reading: Matthew 28:1-10

Tell his disciples that he has risen.

All the gospels were written sometime after the events of the life of Christ. Each was written with a different community in mind and so each has a special character and focus. Each tells the story from a different perspective. There is no single account of the passion and resurrection of Jesus. Together, however, the four gospels offer us a holistic view of this tremendous event.

Here St. Matthew is giving us an account of the resurrection of Jesus to a Christian community that is made up of Jewish converts. Throughout his gospel Matthew tries to show Jesus as the new Moses. All the hopes that the Jewish people had placed in Moses are now found in Christ. The resurrection occurs "on the first day" as is only proper for a "new creation." The resurrection is accompanied by signs and wonders similar to those signs and wonders that had surrounded the appearances of God in the Old Testament. The resurrection is an awesome event, accomplished by the direct intervention of God.

The women did not see the resurrection of Jesus, but they did see the angel in white robes who had rolled back the stone. While the guards fainted, the women received both a message and a mission to announce to the disciples that Jesus was raised from the dead.

It is impossible to tell this story in the ordinary language of human history or judge it with any human criteria. It is an announcement that will change the world and requires poetry.

PURPOSE: We must use our imaginations to picture the meeting of Jesus and Mary.

SUMMARY: While the Sacred Triduum marks the passage to the new covenant, this passage was anticipated in the whole life of Jesus and Mary. It makes their meeting unique.

MUSINGS:

1. Blessed Pope John Paul II on Easter 1983: "The Gospels do not speak to us of any apparition of the Risen Jesus to his mother: this ineffable mystery of joy remains under the veil of a mystical silence. It is certain, however, that she, the first to be redeemed, just as she was in a special way near her Son's cross (Jn 19:25), also had the privileged experience of the Risen Christ, such as to cause in her a most intense joy, unique among that of all other creatures who were saved by the blood of Christ."

2. "Mary is a guide for us in the knowledge of the mysteries of the Lord: and just as in her and with her, we understand the meaning of the cross, so in her and with her we are able to understand the significance of the resurrection, tasting the joy that comes from such an experience."

3. "Mary, in fact, among all creatures, 'believed,' from the very beginning, all that the Word, becoming flesh in her, did in the world for the salvation of the world. In an ascent of exultation based on faith, her joy passed from the '*Magnificat*,' full of hope, to that purest joy, no longer a shadow of decline, over her Son's triumph over sin and death."

4. The Blessed Pope reminds us of the contrast of the two kinds of joy that Mary possessed. The first was the joy of the *Magnificat*, the second the joy of the resurrection. The first was the joy of hope. The second was the joy of possession.

5. The specific images found in the Scriptures for this celebration of many ways by which we may picture Holy Mary: she is the Holy City, the Bride adorned, the place where God dwells; she wipes away every tear; she is the beginning of the new order.

RELATION TO THE EUCHARIST: Who better to accompany us to the celebration of the Eucharist than the risen Christ and his holy mother Mary?

Sources

Revelation: *Guide for the Christian Assembly: A Background Book of the Mass*, 9 vols., ed. Thierry Maertens and Jean Frisque (Notre Dame, IN: Fides Publishers, 1971), IV:162.

Matthew: Ibid., III:328.

Daniel J. Harrington, *The Gospel of Matthew*, Sacra Pagina Series (Collegeville, MN: Liturgical Press, 1991), 408.

Marian Reflections: The Angelus Messages of Pope John Paul II, ed. David O. Brown (Washington, NJ: AMI Press, 1990), 1–9.

16. HOLY MARY, FOUNTAIN OF LIGHT AND LIFE

Exegesis of the First Reading: Acts 2:14a, 36-40a, 41-42

Everyone must be baptized in the name of Jesus Christ.

This short passage is taken from the first recorded homily ever given. In it St. Peter gives us a summary and insight into the whole faith, life, and practice of the early church.

It is the feast of Pentecost, and Peter wastes no time in reminding the crowds that they were responsible for the death of Jesus, this Jesus who is both the Lord and the Messiah. When the audience asks Peter what they are to do, his answer is clear. They are to repent and be baptized. They will receive the gift of the Holy Spirit and the forgiveness of their sins. Luke describes for us the life of that first Christian community, one devoted to the teachings of the apostles, the communal life, breaking of the bread, and prayer.

The meaning of this passage for the church then and now is profound. The sequence we see here is the sequence that is followed even today in the Rite of Christian Initiation of Adults. The rite emphasizes the fundamental elements of our Christian life and practice, that is, teaching, community, Eucharist, and prayer.

Exegesis of the Gospel Reading: John 12:44-50

I, the light, have come into the world.

Chronologically this is the last time Jesus will preach openly to the crowds. In this passage St. John gives us a summary of all the teaching of Jesus found in the Fourth Gospel. Jesus is the one who brings life and light into the world. Jesus brings salvation. Jesus is the one who speaks the words of the Father.

Earlier Jesus had gone into hiding but is now speaking publicly once again. His words are words of salvation. Some will reject his words. This implies a judgment, not a judgment he will give but a judgment people will bring upon themselves.

This is a very complex passage. We must all make the journey from darkness into the light. The passage gives us a résumé of the whole gospel. Jesus is the divine agent who is to replace Moses and the Torah. He is a revealing and judging presence. He reveals the glory of God to the world. Jesus himself is the revelation of the Father, and Jesus himself brings light into the world. He emerges from hiding and darkness to walk in the light.

Jesus introduces a second thought here as well, salvation. He has come into the world to save the world. In John's gospel, salvation means that here and now we possess the divine life. We come to that divine life by listening to and obeying the words of Jesus, who is really speaking the words of the Father.

Exegesis of the Alternate Gospel Reading: John 3:1-6

What is born of the Spirit is spirit.

John's gospel is very integrated and so a word about the context is necessary. In the second chapter, St. John told of the signs, which Jesus performed at Cana and of the temple with the money changers and the promise to rebuild the temple in three days. Here in chapter 3, John recounts the reactions to these signs. The first reaction is that of Nicodemus. Later Jesus will have his exchange with the Samaritan woman at the well, and still later, he will cure the son of the royal official.

Nicodemus had studied the Scriptures to learn about the Messiah. Jesus immediately reminds him, however, that more than study is needed. To know Jesus intimately one needs a change of heart. One undergoes a new birth in faith. A new birth in the Spirit will allow a person to "see." All this implies a profound change, which places a person, by faith, in total dependence on God.

Must one enter the womb again? Nicodemus asks. No, Jesus says, one must be "born of water and Spirit." By the time John was writing this gospel, his audience would understand these words in a way that Nicodemus could not. They would know about being born again of "water and Spirit." By then almost all the followers of Christ would have been baptized.

PURPOSE: Jesus is the light and Mary a bearer of that light.

SUMMARY: The Scriptures are to help us move from the theory in the gospel to the practice in the mission.

MUSINGS:

1. Both the decrees accompanying the publication of this Collection of Masses of the Blessed Virgin Mary give us an excellent overall picture of how the church understands Mary's role in the work of salvation and how the church uses various passages of Scripture to teach us about that role. We note that in each of the selections for this feast, for Mary herself does not appear. What the Scripture is teaching us, however, is exemplified by Mary.

2. Mary was there listening to that first sermon of St. Peter. She had been at prayer with Peter and the rest of the apostles when they received the Holy Spirit just minutes before. As she listened to what Peter had to say, did she wonder if his words about sin related to her?

3. The gift of the Holy Spirit that she had just received with the other disciples was not the first time she had received the Holy Spirit. Did she think back and remember how it all began?

4. We can never know what Mary might have been thinking as she received the gift of the Spirit in such a unique way. Fundamentally, however, the same divine Spirit is operating in us. Of course she was unique and special, but, like us, in need of redemption.

5. Peter, in the first reading, reminded his audience that they had been responsible for the death of Jesus. This gospel was composed at a time when there was great tension between the Jewish and the new Christian communities. Over the centuries this has given rise to a great deal of anti-Semitism. The Jews who called for the death of Jesus were

responsible for themselves. It was and is wrong to blame all the Jews of any age for the death of Jesus.

6. Celebrating Easter in the Northern or Southern Hemisphere will put the sun in different positions in the sky. As it shines, north or south, it illuminates stained glass windows and makes things bright and shining. The Easter celebration takes place in the spring (or fall) when the sun is climbing (or declining) in the sky. The sun changes things. It lets us see. It makes things bright. The gospel today reminds us that Jesus does the same thing for each of us.

7. It is Jesus who is the light. He is like the sun! Jesus is the fountain of light. Jesus is, as well, the source of all life, a new life, a new creation, a new beginning. Therefore, as we call Jesus the fountain of life we remind ourselves that Mary was his mother.

8. It was the disposition of Divine Providence that Jesus, the sun, the light, the life, took his flesh in the Virgin Mary. She was the instrument God had chosen to show us the light and the life. Thus, we may see in Mary a reflected, but real, fountain of light and life.

RELATION TO THE EUCHARIST: As Mary and the apostles received the gift of the Spirit, so we pray for the gift of the Spirit as we approach the Eucharist.

Sources

Acts: *Guide for the Christian Assembly: A Background Book of the Mass*, 9 vols., ed. Thierry Maertens and Jean Frisque (Notre Dame, IN: Fides Publishers, 1971), IV:61, 113.

John A: Ibid., IV:45.

John B: Ibid., IV:50.

The Jerome Biblical Commentary, ed. Raymond E. Brown, Joseph A. Fitzmyer, and Roland E. Murphy (Englewood Cliffs, NJ: Prentice-Hall, 1968).

17. OUR LADY OF THE CENACLE

Exegesis of the First Reading: Acts 1:6-14

You will receive the power of the Holy Spirit.

Luke has given us two books of Sacred Scriptures, the gospel and the Acts of the Apostles. In both of these books, however, St. Luke has a single overarching plan. It is the journeys of Jesus, where in the gospel we see Jesus on his journey to Jerusalem and in Acts we see Jesus send his disciples away from Jerusalem to the whole world. The influence of the gospel message will spread beyond Jerusalem, to Judea and Samaria and then among Gentiles and finally to Rome and the whole world. In effect, Luke is here giving us something of a new annunciation. At the first, God became man in Jesus and came into the world. Jesus died and was raised to live again, and now the disciples of Jesus are to take this message and deliver it to the world.

In the first annunciation the Spirit comes upon Mary. Now, in this second annunciation the Spirit comes upon Mary and the disciples.

Along with the disciples, "the brothers" of Jesus are here as well. There is no longer any evidence of any possible rift between them as we see early in Luke's gospel: "All these devoted themselves with one accord to prayer" with Mary the mother of Jesus (Acts 1:14).

Exegesis of the Gospel Reading: Luke 8:19-21

My mother and my brothers are those who hear the word of God and put it into practice.

We can be certain of this: at one time Mary and the brothers of Jesus went looking for him. This particular incident is related in each of the three Synoptic Gospels: Matthew 12:46-50; Mark 3:31-35; and here in Luke's gospel.

In Matthew's gospel Jesus had been speaking to the crowds about how difficult it would be to follow him. Just then, someone told him that his mother and brothers were looking for him. Jesus offered a universal invitation to kinship with him. Only those who do the will of the Father can be his kin.

Mark was describing the confrontation of Jesus with some of the scribes. The scribes were very concerned about the observance of the law and rituals. Again Jesus lays down the one condition of kinship, discipleship. Only one thing is necessary, to do the will of the Father.

In this passage from St. Luke, Jesus is also relating his parables to the crowds. He had told them about the sower and the seed, about putting one's light on a lamp stand. When he is told that his mother and brothers wish to see him, he gives the same answer he had given in the other gospels: "My mother and my brothers are those / who hear the word of God and act on it."

We are able to see the full significance of these words of Jesus if we move back from this eighth chapter of this gospel to Luke 1:38, where we hear Mary say, "Behold, I am the handmaid of the Lord. / May it be done to me according to your word."

From the very beginning, Mary is one for whom the Father's will always comes first.

Purpose: To present a picture of the first Christian community.

Summary: Mary and the apostles, together in prayer, and receiving the gift of the Spirit, have given us a picture of the first Christian community.

MUSINGS:

1. The structure of Luke's gospel suggests that Jesus makes his way to Jerusalem and then the faith extends from Jerusalem to the whole world.

2. The first Christian community in Jerusalem was not to spend its time looking up to heaven. They had work to do. Soon the Holy Spirit would come upon them, and they were to begin their mission to bring the faith to the world.

3. One thing the apostles shared was a common experience with each other and with Jesus. The end of the first Scripture selection suggests that they likewise shared a common experience with Mary, the mother of Jesus; she was there.

4. It is important to note that "the brothers" of Jesus are here as well. There is no evidence of a possible rift, noted early in Luke's gospel. All that has been healed. "All these devoted themselves with one accord to prayer" with Mary the mother of Jesus.

5. You might try this experiment sometime. Ask a group if they would rather be deaf or blind. Most will answer that they would prefer to have their sight. The reason for this little experiment is to emphasize, by contrast, just how important hearing is for the follower of Christ. Sight is important, but listening gives depth.

6. This particular gospel passage might well be the starting place for greater ecumenical cooperation. There is a single test for discipleship: "those / who hear the word of God and act on it." All share a special kinship with each other and with Jesus. And with Mary.

RELATION TO THE EUCHARIST: Community, prayer, the Spirit: these are the elements we need to celebrate the Eucharist properly.

Sources

Acts: *Guide for the Christian Assembly: A Background Book of the Mass*, 9 vols., ed. Thierry Maertens and Jean Frisque (Notre Dame, IN: Fides Publishers, 1971), IV:228, 251.

The Jerome Biblical Commentary, ed. Raymond E. Brown, Joseph A. Fitzmyer, and Roland E. Murphy (Englewood Cliffs, NJ: Prentice-Hall, 1968).

Gospel: *Guide for the Christian Assembly*, VII:87; VI:95; V:41; II:101.

18. THE BLESSED VIRGIN MARY, QUEEN OF APOSTLES

Exegesis of the First Reading: Acts 1:12-14; 2:1-4

*With one heart the disciples continued in steadfast prayer
with Mary, the mother of Jesus.*

Luke has a preoccupation with Jerusalem. His gospel begins and ends in the temple and with the Spirit, with the appearance of the angel to Zechariah. The gospel is concerned with the journey of Jesus to Jerusalem. Now in the Acts of the Apostles St. Luke takes up the journey of the gospel itself, which under the guidance of the Spirit will make its journey to the ends of the earth.

In the first chapter of Acts, Luke recounted the ascension of the Lord, which was witnessed by the apostles. Now they are back in Jerusalem to begin their first apostolic work. It was to gather in prayer with the brothers of Jesus, some other women, and Mary, the mother of Jesus.

In the second section of this first reading, Luke uses words that seem to reflect the words he had used once before at the annunciation to Mary. "The holy Spirit will come upon you, and the power of the Most High will overshadow you" (Luke 1:35). The "time was fulfilled" for the gift of the Holy Spirit. In the first annunciation the Holy Spirit overshadowed Mary; here the Holy Spirit overshadows the apostles.

Exegesis of the Gospel Reading: John 19:25-27

Woman, this is your son. This is your mother.

How many people were in the small group of followers who were at the foot of the cross? Scholars and artists are not agreed. Certainly Mary the mother of Jesus was there and her sister. The beloved disciple was there and Mary of Magdala. The question is whether the sister of the Blessed Virgin was also the wife of Clopas. We will leave it to the scholars to count the people. We will focus on what we know for sure.

It was perfectly natural for Mary to be at the foot of the cross. We find clues to her presence there back at the marriage feast of Cana. Jesus spoke of the hour that had not yet come at that time and now his hour has come. We may see a clue in her words to the servants at Cana when she told them, "Do whatever he tells you" (John 2:5). Could she do less herself?

The disciple whom Jesus loved was near to him at the Last Supper. Most people believe that this beloved disciple was John, but we cannot be sure. It may also have been John, one of the sons of Zebedee. What is most important is that this disciple was beloved by Jesus so much so that Jesus entrusted his mother to him.

Mary of Magdala seems to have been a good woman devoted to the Lord, living in good circumstances and of unblemished character. She was faithful to him and was at his crucifixion. Especially noteworthy is that she is the first person to whom the risen Lord appeared. These disciples ascended the mountain to stand by his cross and they are now ready to make the adventure down the mountain into the world.

PURPOSE: The story of Jesus is a story for the world.

SUMMARY: Jesus expected his disciples to go into the whole world with his message. They were empowered by the Holy Spirit as Mary was when she began her journey of faith at Nazareth.

MUSINGS:

1. The two readings of this setting point to the two very important elements in the whole gospel story, the death of Jesus on Calvary and the descent of the Holy Spirit on the apostles, the fundamental elements of evangelization.

2. We often see pictures of Mary in the midst of the apostles waiting for the gift of the Holy Spirit. This is a familiar image and portrays an important aspect of Mary's relationship with the apostles. It is not just waiting; it is being ready.

3. To see the depth of what is implied in this title of "Queen of Apostles," we must go back to Cana of Galilee, where Mary met the apostles for the first time and was with them when they first came to believe.

4. Because St. John places Mary at Cana and again on Calvary, we can see the special role of Mary in the mystery of salvation.

5. Later St. Paul will appeal to his own experience to assert his role as an apostle, equal to the twelve. Because of Mary's experience at Cana and on Calvary, may we by analogy then call her the Queen of Apostles?

6. Our focus is on Mary but she is joined by Mary of Magdala, a woman to whom Jesus would appear after the resurrection. She ranks with the apostles even if not so entitled.

7. When we reflect on the full relationship of Mary and the apostles, a relationship begun at Cana and at Pentecost, we must see that there is more here than an occasion for a lovely group picture. It offers us a model of belief and discipleship and a membership par excellence in a believing apostolic community.

RELATION TO THE EUCHARIST: Dare we imagine that we join the company of the apostles as we approach the altar?

Sources

Marian Reflections: The Angelus Messages of Pope John Paul II, ed. David O. Brown (Washington, NJ: AMI Press, 1990), 62.

Guide for the Christian Assembly: A Background Book of the Mass, 9 vols., ed. Thierry Maertens and Jean Frisque (Notre Dame, IN: Fides Publishers, 1971), IV:251.

Marian Reflections, 1, 43, 59, 138, 139.

ORDINARY TIME

The Masses found in this section celebrate the work that God accomplishes in Mary as well as her relationship to Christ and the church.

This section is further divided into three subsections. The first group derives their titles from the Sacred Scriptures. The second group refers to Mary's cooperation in the spiritual growth of the faithful. The third group reflects her compassionate intercession.

SECTION 1

This set of Masses celebrates Mary under titles that are taken from the Sacred Scriptures or that highlight Mary's connection with the church.

19. HOLY MARY, MOTHER OF THE LORD

Exegesis of the First Reading: 1 Chronicles 15:3-4, 15-16; 16:1-2

Mary, whose womb bore the Lord, is hailed as the ark of the Lord.

Moses originally constructed the ark of the covenant at God's command. It contained some of the manna that the Lord provided for his people while they were in the desert and the staff of Moses by which the Lord led his people to freedom. Most of all it held the stone tablets on which the law of the Lord was written. The ark was revered because of what it contained. It was a special sign of the presence and providence of God among his people.

When David brought the ark to the holy city Jerusalem and later still when Solomon installed it in the temple, it was always the sign of the presence of God with his people. The book of Chronicles was probably compiled sometime after the exile to renew and revive the faith of the people in the continuing presence of God among his chosen people.

This passage is also used on the feast of the Assumption of the Blessed Virgin Mary.

Exegesis of the Gospel Reading: Luke 1:39-47

Blessed is the fruit of your womb.

As we reflect on the images evoked by the readings of this feast and especially the images given to us by St. Luke, we can see, sprinkled in each, references to the books of the Torah, the Chronicles, Kings, Samuel, and many of the prophets. Jesus is the fulfillment of the Scriptures and of all the prophecies. This is what Luke and all the evangelists tell us.

Mary is the instrument that God used to effect his presence among us. When Mary travels to visit Elizabeth, Elizabeth is filled with the Holy Spirit. Even the child in her womb is touched (Gen 25:22). Elizabeth commends the obedience of Mary with words that again echo the words spoken by the people in the desert of Sinai. In the last verse, Mary reminds us that whatever graces she may have, these graces are from the Lord.

PURPOSE: Jesus is the Lord and his mother is Mary.

SUMMARY: The overarching message of all the Scriptures is that God is with us. To which we add, Mary is his mother.

MUSINGS:

1. The image of the ark of the covenant as a sign of the Blessed Virgin Mary is especially vivid. The ark contained the relics of the time the chosen people lived in the desert. It held the staff of Moses, some of the manna, and, most especially, the tablets on which the law of the Lord was written. Mary held in her womb the very Son of God.

2. King David pitched a tent and set the ark within it. The Latin word for tent is tabernacle. That is why the rubric calls for our tabernacles to be veiled. Today we do not place a sign of the presence of God in our tabernacles; we place the Son of God, the Lord Jesus himself.

3. What is the fundamental basis for our devotion to Mary? The fathers at Vatican II began their treatment of Mary, in chapter 8 in the Dogmatic Constitution on the Church (*Lumen Gentium* 53), with these

words: "The Virgin Mary, who at the message of the angel received the Word of God in her heart and in her body and brought forth life to the world."

4. The fathers of the council tell us, therefore, that the "function" of Mary is the source of the entire honor we give to her. The first time she exercised this function was when she rose in haste to visit Elizabeth.

5. May we express our disappointment that the first reading left out the picture of David dancing before the ark. Think of the passion and zeal he brought to his devotion. Dare we say that John danced before the Lord as King David had danced before the ark (2 Sam 6:16)?

6. We might remember the words of Isaiah (35:5-6) of the responses given to the coming of the Savior:

> Then the eyes of the blind shall see,
> 　　and the ears of the deaf be opened;
> Then the lame shall leap like a stag,
> 　　and the mute tongue sing for joy.

RELATION TO THE EUCHARIST: As we approach the Eucharist, might we not modify the words of Elizabeth as we wonder how it is that the Lord would come to us?

Sources

Guide for the Christian Assembly: A Background Book of the Mass, 9 vols., ed. Thierry Maertens and Jean Frisque (Notre Dame, IN: Fides Publishers, 1971), IX:60.

Marian Reflections: The Angelus Messages of Pope John Paul II, ed. David O. Brown (Washington, NJ: AMI Press, 1990), 14, 30, 31, 33, 50, 64, 67–69, 94, 102, 107, 110.

20. HOLY MARY, THE NEW EVE

Exegesis of the First Reading: Revelation 21:1-5a

I saw the new Jerusalem, as beautiful as a bride
all dressed for her husband.

The author of the book of Revelation seems to be reading the book of Genesis as he composes this passage. We find here all the elements of the Garden of Eden. However, it is a new and special garden. The earth and the garden were created by the Lord, and Adam and Eve took up their residence there until they failed and were banished. The beauty of the garden was defiled by their disobedience. Yet even as they were expelled from the garden, they were given hope (Gen 3). Now, in the final chapter of the New Testament, that hope is revealed in all its fullness. Here we find the promise of a new garden, a new heaven, and a new earth. Every tear will be wiped away. There will be no more death or mourning, no wailing, no pain. Creation is renewed and refashioned in a way that befits a redeemed humanity (Isa 65:17; 66:22).

The first reading is a passage that the fathers of the church have always read as referring to Mary. Certain scholars, however, do not always agree. The General Introduction to this collection reminds us that the events, figures, and symbols foretell or suggest in a wonderful manner the life and mission of Mary. It is for this very purpose that they were chosen.

Exegesis of the Gospel Reading: Luke 1:26-38

Hail, full of grace.

This is the second most frequently used passage in this entire collection. The most frequently used gospel selection is from John (2:1-11), which is given as the alternative gospel for this celebration. Luke tells us of the coming of the Messiah who is the author of the new creation. This passage from Luke, where the coming Messiah is announced, is very appropriate for this celebration, especially when we refer to the first reading, where the idea of the new creation is more explicit. God is about to realize, in Mary, the mystery of the promise of the Old Testament. She is to vanquish the enemy by crushing his head (see Judg 5:24; Gen 3:15).

Exegesis of the Alternate Gospel Reading: John 2:1-11

The mother of Jesus said to the attendants: Do whatever he tells you.

As indicated in the previous exegesis, this gospel selection is the one most frequently used in the Collection of Masses of the Blessed Virgin Mary. It is one of the pivotal passages of John's gospel. The themes, signs, and symbols, so important in John's gospel, appear here for the first time. The "day," the "hour," the sign, water, glory, "Woman," which we find here, will appear again and again.

Mary takes the lead as this story unfolds. Surprisingly, she receives in return what seems to be an unexpectedly sharp response from Jesus. A distinct distance seems to be established between Jesus and his mother. Jesus is of one world, Mary of another.

Probably Mary has no knowledge of the divine world in which Jesus exists. She turns from this seeming rebuke to instruct the servants that they should do everything Jesus asks of them. She has an unconditional trust in the efficacy of his word. She is the first person to show in action that the correct response to the presence of Jesus is fidelity to his word. The servants do as Mary instructed them. Her instructions lead to the miracle, the sign of his glory, and then to an expression of faith by the disciples. His glory was manifested as a consequence of an unconditioned acceptance of his word.

The steward thinks that this is the high point of the feast; the hour has come because of the good wine. Rather the "hour" will be much later.

PURPOSE: To establish Mary's place in the new creation.

SUMMARY: This is the start of something new and so all the characters must have their places and their functions.

MUSINGS:

1. This feast of Mary, the New Eve, addresses just one small facet of a great story. When we speak of her as the New Eve, we are not simply connecting her to the Eve in the garden. It is much more than changing *EVA* to *AVE*, as lovely as that image may be. Rather, as she is mother of Jesus, the Messiah, so she is the mother of the church, the New Eve in the new creation.

2. As St. John carefully counted the days since Jesus was baptized in the Jordan, this is the seventh day. Now is the time for a new creation, and a new creation story and a turning point in the history of salvation.

3. We do not like to think of the words of Jesus to his mother as a rebuke. But what else can we think? He spoke sharply to Mary. For her part, she responded as all of us must, with trust.

4. The people in the desert of Sinai, after they had received the commandments from Moses, shouted, "We will do everything the Lord has told us" (Exod 24:3). Now Mary, with faith and trust, suggests that the servants at the wedding do the same thing; they are to do whatever he tells them.

5. The Lord is no longer speaking from Mount Sinai or from Cana in Galilee. He speaks to us now from our real world in our real situation. The response of the people in the desert and our response must be the same. We are to do whatever he tells us.

6. The stories of creation that we find in the book of Genesis initiate the story of salvation. Those stories, however, do not tell us of the specific Christian understanding of creation. Paul speaks of a "new creation" in Christ (Gal 6:15; 2 Cor 5:17). We are all created in Christ. In him we live and move and have our being.

7. The "new creation" was initiated "when the fullness of time had come, God sent his Son, born of a woman, born under the law, to ransom those under the law, so that we might receive adoption" (Gal 4:4). That "woman" was the New Eve, Mary.

RELATION TO THE EUCHARIST: As we approach the altar we are never alone.

Sources

Pope Pius XII, *Mediator Dei*, encyclical (November 20, 1947).

The Jerome Biblical Commentary, ed. Raymond E. Brown, Joseph A. Fitzmyer, and Roland E. Murphy (Englewood Cliffs, NJ: Prentice-Hall, 1968).

The Collegeville Bible Commentary, ed. Dianne Bergant and Robert J. Karris (Collegeville, MN: Liturgical Press, 1989).

Do Whatever He Tells You: Reflections and Proposals for Promoting Marian Devotion (Rome: General Curia OSM, 1983), 69.

Servants of the *Magnificat*: The Canticle of the Blessed Virgin and Consecrated Life (Rome: General Curia OSM, 1996), 38.

Christopher O'Donnell, *At Worship with Mary: A Pastoral and Theological Study* (Wilmington, DE: Michael Glazier, 1988), 119.

Marian Reflections: The Angelus Messages of Pope John Paul II, ed. David O. Brown (Washington, NJ: AMI Press, 1990), 27, 91.

Do Whatever He Tells You, 26, 76, 45, 101.

21. THE HOLY NAME OF THE BLESSED VIRGIN MARY

Exegesis of the First Reading: Sirach 24:17-21

Remembrance of me is a legacy to future generations.

Commentators tell us that Sirach was writing to the Jews of his day who were being drawn to an alien, Greek philosophy. Don't wander away, he says, you will not find wisdom out there. True wisdom is found in Israel. It buds forth delights; it is sweeter than honey or the honeycomb. Drawn to its sweetness, we will always desire more. And there is obedience and service as well.

The General Introduction to this collection of Masses tells us that particular Scripture selections are chosen to reflect the life mission of Mary or her relation to Christ. They are also chosen to illustrate the virtues that flourished in Mary.

Exegesis of the Gospel Reading: Luke 1:26-38

The virgin's name was Mary.

When this passage was used in other celebrations of Mary, we indicated that this is an example of a specific literary device called "midrash" in which every aspect of the passage, every word and phrase, is filled with associations to other parts of the Scriptures. Thus, whenever there is an "angel" found in an episode, we know that the passage is both prophetic and eschatological. It is prophetic when it sets a standard that we must achieve. It is eschatological when it points to the future. In this passage, the titles once given to Jerusalem are now transferred to Mary. Before the feast of Pentecost, it is possible that Mary did not understand fully the divine mission of her Son. She will "ponder" these words as she will ponder other words and actions of Jesus. This does not diminish her in any way. She is full of grace, as were Ruth and Esther in Old Testament.

The titles given to Jesus, "great," "Son of the Most High," "Messiah," "throne of David," indicate the high expectations Israel had for him.

PURPOSE: When we use a person's name, we imply everything there is in that person.

SUMMARY: The whole passage, celebration, collection is summed up with the words "and the virgin's name was Mary."

MUSINGS:

1. The *Catechism of the Catholic Church* (par. 721) paraphrases this section of the book of Sirach and Proverbs 8: "Mary, the all-holy ever-virgin Mother of God, is the masterwork of the mission of the Son and the Spirit in the fullness of time."

2. "For the first time in the plan of salvation and because his Spirit had prepared her, the Father found the *dwelling place* where his Son and his Spirit could dwell among men" (ibid.).

3. "In this sense the Church's Tradition has often read the most beautiful texts on wisdom in relation to Mary. (cf. Prov 8:1–9:6; Sir 24) Mary is acclaimed and represented in the liturgy as the 'Seat of Wisdom'" (ibid.).

4. "In her, the 'wonders of God' that the Spirit was to fulfill in Christ and the Church began to be manifested" (ibid.). Truly she buds forth delights like the vine; truly her blossoms become fruit fair and rich. Such is the holy name of Mary.

5. In passing we might say that in the reading from Sirach we find the inspiration of the hymn of St. Bernard about the sweetness of the name of Jesus. No doubt this is the reason for its use on this feast of the name of Mary.

RELATION TO THE EUCHARIST: The angel addresses the mother of the Lord with her name Mary. It should be on our lips as we approach the Lord.

Sources

The Jerome Biblical Commentary, ed. Raymond E. Brown, Joseph A. Fitzmyer, and Roland E. Murphy (Englewood Cliffs, NJ: Prentice-Hall, 1968).

The Collegeville Bible Commentary, ed. Dianne Bergant and Robert J. Karris (Collegeville, MN: Liturgical Press, 1989).

Guide for the Christian Assembly: A Background Book of the Mass, 9 vols., ed. Thierry Maertens and Jean Frisque (Notre Dame, IN: Fides Publishers, 1971), I:146; IX:60.

22. HOLY MARY, HANDMAID OF THE LORD

Exegesis of the First Reading: 1 Samuel 1:24-28; 2:1-2, 4-8

I stood praying to the Lord, and the Lord granted my request.

This selection presumes that we remember the whole story of Hannah in the Old Testament. She and her husband Elkanah had come to the temple to pray to the Lord for a child. Her deeply felt emotional prayer to the Lord prompted the high priest to think she was drunk. Her prayers were answered, however, and now, a year later, she is again in the temple. This time she is there to offer her profound thanks to the Lord for the blessings the Lord had given her. She will do something more. She will now return to the Lord the gift she had received. The sacrifices that her husband was offering are not nearly as important as the sentiments of gratitude she expresses in her prayers. She knows God has control of our human destiny. She acknowledges this and gives thanks. She shows us how to pray.

Her words, the phrases she uses as well as the sentiments with which she expresses her gratitude, will later be echoed by Mary in her *Magnificat*.

Exegesis of the Gospel Reading: Luke 1:26-38

Behold, the handmaid of the Lord.

This is one of the most important passages of the Scriptures.

Greek scholars help us to see more clearly all of what the Lord is revealing to us in this passage. "Grace" in Luke's gospel is always associated with both joy and wisdom. Here St. Luke is suggesting that the emphasis must be placed on God who fills Mary with grace. She is the object of God's favor. The tenses of the verbs, according to those scholars, seem to indicate that this has been true for some time.

As a result, these words of the angel constitute the most impressive salutation in the whole Bible. Luke is not talking about a vision. The angel is communicating a message face-to-face. We can see this when we contrast this greeting with other similar greetings. Both Joseph and Zechariah learned of God's will only in dreams.

When the angel speaks to Mary about her child, he uses language that has been used in the Scriptures to express the presence of God among his people. He will be "great," "Son of the Most High," "holy," "the Son of God." These titles are taken from the Psalms and the prophets. All indicate the saving presence of the Lord among his people.

We must remember that this passage is not a newspaper account of what happened at the annunciation. It is a divine revelation about our salvation. Strange as it may seem, we might say that we understand this passage and the message of the angel better than Mary herself did. We are able to look back with faith at this scene and the whole life story of Jesus. We see the whole picture. Mary, of course, with her people, looked forward in faith to the coming Messiah. Ours is hindsight. We see better than she that this is the unique moment of the Messiah's arrival. We know who the Messiah is. Mary, on her part, was ready. She was open to the divine will. "May it be done to me."

We might mention also that Bl. Pope John Paul II used the expression "joyful" instead of "hail" as he began the "Ave." The greeting includes a sense of joy, which is missing in the simple word "hail." Here, as in most of the Scriptures, there is more to the message than just the words.

PURPOSE: Once we know who Mary is, then we need to know her function.

SUMMARY: Both in the Hebrew Scriptures and now in the Christian Scriptures, the Lord God used women as his instruments.

MUSINGS:

1. There are times when people of goodwill ask, "Is it in the Scriptures?" They may be asking about Mary's immaculate conception or her assumption into heaven. The literal answer is "No, it is not." Yet, if we reflect, if we ponder the words as Mary pondered over the words, if we pray over this particular part of the Scriptures, as Mary prayed, could we not in all truth say, "Yes, it is somehow in the Scriptures"?

2. The greeting of the angel tells us something about Mary even if we know nothing else. She is blessed by the Lord. The Lord is with her already. She is already full of grace. She is comforted even as she is troubled by an angel of the Lord. Talk about special!

3. If being visited by an angel were not enough, "[t]he holy Spirit will come upon you, / and the power of the Most High will overshadow you."

As the cloud overshadowed the people in the desert, as the cloud filled the temple of Jerusalem, now this woman of Nazareth is overshadowed by the Holy Spirit. What was illustrated by a sign in the Old Testament is now accomplished in Mary (See Mass no. 23).

4. There is more. "Behold, I am the handmaid of the Lord. / May it be done to me according to your word." We learn so much more about her in these words. She knows who she is and is in control of herself. She is mature—she is adult, no matter what her age. She is decisive, saying, I am here, I am open. Do it, Lord. Work your will, I am ready.

RELATION TO THE EUCHARIST: What better attitude for celebrating the Eucharist than "May it be done to me according to your word."

Sources

Navarre Bible, *Saint Luke* (Dublin: Four Courts Press, 1987), 36.
Guide for the Christian Assembly: A Background Book of the Mass, 9 vols., ed. Thierry Maertens and Jean Frisque (Notre Dame, IN: Fides Publishers, 1971), I:142; II:70; IX:25, 90.

23. THE BLESSED VIRGIN MARY, TEMPLE OF THE LORD

Exegesis of the First Reading: 1 Kings 8:1, 3-7, 9-11

A cloud filled the temple of the Lord God.

The choice of this reading illustrates once again the explanation of the General Introduction to this whole set of Mass texts. The Old and New Testaments together constitute a single corpus that is permeated by the mystery of Christ. Therefore, events, figures, and symbols foretell or suggest in a wonderful manner the life and mission of Mary.

In the book of Exodus, the Lord God said to Moses, "They are to make a sanctuary for me, that I may dwell in their midst. According to all that I show you regarding the pattern of the tabernacle and the pattern of its furnishings, so you are to make it" (25:8-9). Moses then constructed the ark of the covenant. The people carried it through the desert, across the Jordan, and frequently into battle. They were very devoted to the ark. It was for them the sign of the Lord's presence.

When things were more settled, King David brought the ark to Jerusalem with great solemnity. In this passage King Solomon carries the ark to the temple of the Lord that he had built. The Lord has taken possession of his house. The elders carry it into the holy of holies. In the last verse, a cloud fills the temple of the Lord. The cloud is something visible, a sensible sign of the presence of God. It had sheltered the Israelites from the desert heat during the forty years. The cloud is called the "glory" of the Lord.

Exegesis of the Alternate First Reading: Revelation 21:1-5a

Here God lives among his people.

At the time that the book of Revelation was written, sometime after the year 70, Jerusalem had fallen to the Romans and its temple was destroyed. Now the Lord is reminding the people who had been dispersed and sent into exile that they have not been forgotten. Rather, waiting for them is a new and eternal Jerusalem come down from heaven. The sign of hope, the temple of Jerusalem, which had been given to them in the past, may be lost, but there is a new sign of hope. It will come from a new heaven. The old heavens will have passed away. There will be a heavenly Jerusalem. The covenant itself will be a new covenant. Most important of all, just as in the original covenant, God lived with his people, so now, in the new covenant, God will continue to dwell with his people.

Exegesis of the Gospel Reading: Luke 1:26-38

The power of the Most High will overshadow you.

This same passage was used in the previous Mass formula, Holy Mary, Handmaid of the Lord. What was said there may be repeated here.

Scholarship suggests that the infancy narratives of Luke's gospel were written very early and are of Jewish origin. When the archangel Gabriel (Dan 9:21) had delivered a message to Daniel the prophet, his message was both prophetic and eschatological. We may understand the message to Mary in the same way, prophetic and eschatological. It challenges us in the present (prophetic) and it will remind us of the end times (eschatological).

When the angel made the announcement to Zechariah, the father of John the Baptist, it was in the temple. The annunciation to Mary, however, is in Nazareth, a long way away from Jerusalem. The whole structure of Luke's gospel is to follow the journey of Jesus up to Jerusalem, and then in the Acts of the Apostles, to follow the journey of faith to the whole world. We are able to see prefigured in the journey of Jesus from Nazareth to Bethlehem to Jerusalem the later public journey of Jesus to Jerusalem.

In this passage also, the angel is transferring the privileges of the temple of Jerusalem to Mary. Twice in this passage Luke refers to Mary as virgin. In Hebrew, the name Mary means "Exalted one."

PURPOSE: To show that Mary was made exactly according to the "pattern" the Lord shows us.

SUMMARY: The sign of God's presence in the Hebrew Scriptures was the ark and the temple. There is a new "presence" and so a new "ark" and a new "temple."

MUSINGS:

1. Our faith rests on the incarnation, when Jesus took flesh and dwelt among us. As John's gospel puts it, "And the Word became flesh / and made his dwelling among us" (1:14). Mary was the place of his dwelling among us.

2. The expression "glory" is frequently used as an attribute of God but is also seen in a sign. So the cloud mentioned at the end of the first reading is that kind of sign. Ezekiel will also use the same word, "glory," and the same sign, the cloud, to indicate the presence of God among us (Ezek 10:2).

3. The creation stories with which we are all familiar from the book of Genesis are not the Christian creation story. These stories of Genesis are vivid with descriptions we can remember and characters and works that serve to explain in story and myth the origins of our physical world. But they are not the Christian story. Our understanding of creation is very different. It is built up from insights from John's gospel, the book of Revelation, and Paul's letter to the Galatians.

4. The Christian "creation story" is called the "new creation." As the book of Genesis begins with "In the beginning . . ." so the Christian creation story begins "In the beginning . . ." but it adds "was the Word"

(John 1:1). It begins with the Word, which will become flesh and dwell among us as Jesus. This is what St. Paul meant when he spoke of "when the fullness of time had come, God sent his Son, born of a woman" (Gal 4:4).

5. Then we consider the image given in the book of Revelation: "Behold, God's dwelling is with the human race." For nine months, literally, Mary was the temple of the Lord.

6. For us, the world has no real meaning without Christ. What good to have been born if we were not redeemed as well?

7. God's wisdom created this world and permeates it. It is this spirit that the Scriptures praise. When, however, the Lord God began to dwell with the human race in a human form, the Lord God did so by taking up residence in Mary. She is indeed "the temple of the Lord."

RELATION TO THE EUCHARIST: We remember that Mary carried Jesus in her womb as we approach the Eucharist to receive him.

Sources

Guide for the Christian Assembly: A Background Book of the Mass, 9 vols., ed. Thierry Maertens and Jean Frisque (Notre Dame, IN: Fides Publishers, 1971), I:146; II:17.
The Christian creation story: Walter Brennan, OSM, "Rethinking Marian Theology: The New Creation," *Milltown Studies* 35 (Spring 1995).

24. THE BLESSED VIRGIN MARY, SEAT OF WISDOM

Exegesis of the First Reading: Proverbs 8:22-31

Mary, Seat of Wisdom.

Frequently, we must use poetry to say things that otherwise cannot be said. This passage is poetry. This same passage is used on the feast of the Mystery of the Most Holy Trinity. At the time it was written, the author was looking back at the history of the Hebrew people, the children of God, and saw that, despite their great accomplishments, each in turn had died. When he looked forward, the vision was clouded. "Is there nothing?" he asked. The people began to reflect that it was the Lord who had created all things. In the course of their reflections, they began to use a poetic figure of speech, personification. They began to ascribe attributes and reflections as though the Lord God were human. They remembered their kings and used the images that had reflected the splendor of those kings. Through these images and metaphors, they were able to see the magnificence of the universe in a new light and realized that it was created by the Lord God. God inspired them to write and sing about it.

In this passage it is as though we have the image of a little child playing before the Lord, giving delight to the Lord who watches over Wisdom.

We take these words that were originally applied to Wisdom and apply them to Mary, in whose womb the Word would become man.

Exegesis of the Alternate First Reading: Sirach 21:1-4, 8-12, 18-21

Mary, Seat of Wisdom.

Here again we have a beautiful, poetic passage. It may be the most beautiful of several similar passages. What is surprising about this very flowery passage is that Sirach is speaking about the law. We frequently think of the law as harsh and static. For the Hebrew people, however, who received the law from the Lord, the *law* was beautiful. It too was seen as a sign of God's presence among his people. It was seen as the instrument of God working among his people, a people chosen by God. Again, part of the theme is that it is in Israel that the Lord God "fixed my abode."

Exegesis of the Gospel Reading: Matthew 2:1-12

Entering the house, they saw the child with Mary, his mother.

This gospel passage was used in the Mass of The Blessed Virgin Mary and the Epiphany of the Lord (no. 6). We may repeat here what was said there. Astrology was very important in ancient times, and in the period between 11 BC and 2 BC a number of extraordinary events took place. The visit by the magi, therefore, need not be considered only a legend. It could easily have happened. People all over the world were expecting great things. They were waiting for a golden age. They were not Jews. In St. Matthew's account, therefore, we find the visit of the magi as the first sign of the universal kingdom of Christ. What is only legend is the number "three." This number is inferred from the number of gifts that the Scriptures describe and to which there is some significance depending on their interpretation. That they may have been kings was not considered until much later.

The Scriptures are best illustrated and best understood by the Scriptures. As Matthew tells us the story about the wicked King Herod, we see a parallel to the book of Numbers where Balaam is asked to curse Israel (Num 22:2-4). He refuses. Later Balaam actually speaks of a star rising in Jacob (Num 24:17). The parallel is clear. Herod wishes harm for the newborn child and is thwarted in his attempt by the star that rises in Jacob.

Exegesis of the Alternate Gospel Reading: Luke 2:15b-19

Mary treasured all these things and pondered them in her heart.

The words that St. Luke uses in this chapter, "savior," "firstborn," "Lord," already indicate that he is looking forward and thinking in terms of the paschal mystery. Mary, on her part, reflects on these things because the birth of Jesus signals the beginning, manifestation, and announcement of the paschal mystery. In the infancy stories Luke is telling us in anticipation much of what will be unfolded little by little later in the gospel.

Here, as in other places in Luke's gospel, we see "amazed" and "praising" used whenever Jesus is revealed. The words used to describe the shepherds will be used later to describe the apostles of the risen Christ (Luke 24:41; Acts 2:11).

Exegesis of the Second Alternate Gospel Reading: Luke 10:38-42

Mary chose the better part.

The Mary of this gospel passage is not the Blessed Virgin. Rather she, Martha, and Lazarus are a family very close to Jesus. Jesus had just finished telling the story of the Good Samaritan and the importance of good works. Now, it is almost as though he wishes to balance out that message by emphasizing the value of contemplation. Both are necessary.

This passage fits very well with the importance that Bl. Pope John Paul II places on the role of women in the new evangelization. Jesus breaks through the bans and prohibitions of his time to show that the Gospel is for all.

PURPOSE: Hearing the ancient Scriptures with Christian ears, we hear songs of Mary.

SUMMARY: All that is good and holy we are able to find in the Scriptures and to turn into praise of Mary's part in the history of salvation.

MUSINGS:

1. We do not know much for sure about the magi except that they certainly were seekers.

2. In the episode of the magi who come from the East to offer homage to the Messiah, we see not only the call of all nations to the faith but also the function of the church following the example of Mary: to present Christ to all peoples and to become a place of encounter with him.

3. It is probable that the evangelist, when writing the episode of the adoration of the magi, took inspiration from Isaiah 60:1-9, the song that celebrates Jerusalem as the center of the universe. In preparing his account, however, he made significant changes. Jerusalem, the City-Mother upon whom the glory of the Lord shines, is replaced by Mary-Mother on whose knees sits the Child. In place of the Lord to whom all the nations offer homage, there is the Child Jesus who receives the homage and adoration of the magi.

4. Mary and the magi show Mary's function in the church, to present Jesus to all who seek him.

5. This meeting and adoration did not take place in the old Jerusalem. No, it was in the "house" of Bethlehem, which may be seen as an image of the church.

6. Note that when they entered the house, they found the Child and his mother. This is true whenever people find the Child, they find his mother. This is the foundation of all our devotion to Mary.

RELATION TO THE EUCHARIST: We are like children playing before the Lord as we approach the Eucharist.

Sources

Do Whatever He Tells You: Reflections and Proposals for Promoting Marian Devotion (Rome: General Curia OSM, 1983), 46.

The Jerome Biblical Commentary, ed. Raymond E. Brown, Joseph A. Fitzmyer, and Roland E. Murphy (Englewood Cliffs, NJ: Prentice-Hall, 1968).

Pope John Paul II, *Christifideles Laici,* post-synodal apostolic exhortation (December 30, 1998).

Guide for the Christian Assembly: A Background Book of the Mass, 9 vols., ed. Thierry Maertens and Jean Frisque (Notre Dame, IN: Fides Publishers, 1971), I:187, 203, 254, 278; IV:316.

25. THE BLESSED VIRGIN MARY, IMAGE AND MOTHER OF THE CHURCH

I

Exegesis of the First Reading: Genesis 3:9-15, 20

I will put enmity between your offspring and her offspring.

Knowing where we come from helps us determine the direction of our journey. So the story of Adam and Eve is not just about where we came from. It gives us an important insight into where we are headed.

In the garden, Adam and Eve enjoyed an intimacy with God. When that intimacy was broken by their sin, the loss was shattering. They were frightened and helpless. They knew they had done wrong. Adam tried to excuse himself by suggesting that it was God's fault since it was God himself who had given the woman to Adam. Then Eve blamed the serpent. The Lord God cursed the serpent as a reminder to Adam and Eve of the evil they had done.

We must note two important nuances of this story. One, it was the Lord God who came to the garden and sought them out. Two, even as the Lord curses the serpent, there is a note of future hope. God is always on the side of the creature he has created.

Exegesis of the Gospel Reading: John 19:25-27

Woman, this is your son. This is your mother.

An extended treatment of the passage from John's gospel will be found at the exegesis in Mass 11, The Blessed Virgin Mary at the Foot of the Cross, I.

Here we add a quote from the Introduction to the Lectionary of Mass formulas of the Blessed Virgin: "Standing at the foot of the cross (see John 19:25), she accepted the words of her Son, who, before he died, entrusted his beloved disciple to her maternal care (see John 19:26). Mary also obeyed the command the risen Lord gave to his apostles, to stay in the city until they had been endowed with power from on high (see Luke 24:49); she remained in Jerusalem and, with one accord continuing in prayer with the apostles, awaited with faith the gift of the Holy Spirit" (par. 8).

PURPOSE: Thus, these Scriptures symbolize and emphasize the role of Mary in the church.

SUMMARY: All salvation is based on faith and hope. Mary, more than any other sign, exemplified this hope.

MUSINGS:

1. Scholars tell us that there is no explicit Mariological reference found in the passage of Genesis that we use on this feast. On the other hand, we do find the note of hope introduced in these first pages of the Scriptures. This note of hope sets the course for all salvation history. We see Mary as an instrument of that hope.

2. For over a thousand years the Christian community has been saying and singing the Salve, the Hail Holy Queen. In it we address both Eve and Mary as mother, with Mary our life, our sweetness, and our hope as well.

3. We never see Mary in isolation. We always see her in relation to her Son Jesus. This is how the fathers of Vatican II treat her in the council document *Lumen Gentium*. Mary of Nazareth is the woman in whom the symbol of Eve, "the mother of all the living" (Gen 3:20), comes to fulfillment in the order of grace. The Catholic Church, taught by the Holy Spirit, honors her with filial affection and devotion as most beloved mother.

4. The council understands Mary's cooperation in the work of salvation in terms of a maternal role: the "motherhood of Mary in the order of grace continues uninterruptedly from the consent which she joyfully gave at the Annunciation and which she sustained, without wavering, beneath the cross until the eternal fulfillment of all the elect" (O'Donnell, *At Worship with Mary*).

5. Pope John Paul II develops the same theme on Easter Sunday, 1983, when he says, "Mary is the one who 'cooperated,' as the Second Vatican Council says, 'in an utterly singular way in the Savior's work of restoring supernatural life to souls, by her obedience, faith and hope and burning charity' (*Lumen Gentium*). And now she cares for the brethren of her son who still journey on earth surrounded by dangers and difficulties, until they are led to their happy fatherland" (Brown, *Marian Reflections*).

6. Mary is our model, image, and mother, even today.

RELATION TO THE EUCHARIST: The example of Mary's faith keeps us company as we approach the Eucharist.

Sources

Marian Reflections: The Angelus Messages of Pope John Paul II, ed. David O. Brown (Washington, NJ: AMI Press, 1990), 77, 79, 99.

Christopher O'Donnell, *At Worship with Mary: A Pastoral and Theological Study* (Wilmington, DE: Michael Glazier, 1988).

Collection of Masses of the Blessed Virgin Mary, Vol. II, Lectionary.

Guide for the Christian Assembly: A Background Book of the Mass, 9 vols., ed. Thierry Maertens and Jean Frisque (Notre Dame, IN: Fides Publishers, 1971), I:32.

26. THE BLESSED VIRGIN MARY, IMAGE AND MOTHER OF THE CHURCH

II

Exegesis of the First Reading: Acts 1:12-14

With one heart the disciples continued in steadfast prayer with Mary, the mother of Jesus.

On September 25, 1983, Bl. Pope John Paul II, in his *Angelus* message, spoke of Mary and her place in the early Christian community. He imagined the scene of Mary and the apostles as it is shown in this passage of the Acts of the Apostles. He likewise connected it with the scene at Cana. The pope's purpose was to show how Mary must animate the church today as she did the early church: "For us too, disciples of the Lord, poverty of spirit amounts to unconditional obedience to his Gospel. It is an education of the heart, which Paul asks for in these words: 'Your attitude must be that of Christ' (Phil 2:5; cf. Mt 11:28-29; Jas 1:21)" (Brown, *Marian Reflections*).

Reflecting on the documents of Vatican II, the pope said, "The same social question, understood as just distribution of goods, both economic and moral, depends as much as ever on the same kind of poverty. Sincere compliance with Christ's word does not tolerate the shame of injustice, of oppression. The early community of Jerusalem, to which Mary belonged (Acts 1:14), 'devoted themselves to the Apostles' instructions and the communal life, to the breaking of bread and the prayers' (Acts 2:42), and as a result of this evangelical fervor, there was no one in need among them (Acts 2:4-5; 4:32, 3-35; cf. Dt 15:4 and 2 Cor 8:13) . . . 'May Christ stir up Mary's poverty in us!' Then the power of his Spirit will give free rein to the 'great things' of the Redemption. Then we will be blessed, because ours is the Kingdom of Heaven" (cf. Mt 5:3) (ibid.).

Exegesis of the Gospel Reading: John 2:1-11

The mother of Jesus was there. And his disciples believed in him.

Biblical commentaries remind us that in the three places where St. John refers to Mary, he never uses her name. He always treats her symbolically. In this passage, Jesus attends the wedding with his disciples, who, because of this first miracle, will come to believe in him. Here, at Cana, the disciples gather around him. In chapter 19, at the crucifixion, all the disciples, except John, have abandoned Jesus. Mary, "the mother of Jesus," however, is present on both occasions.

John in his gospel carefully marks the days in chapters 1 and 2. Cana is the seventh day. As in the book of Genesis, the seven days of creation are finished. Cana now marks the beginning of a new week, a new creation.

Mary is mother in the new creation, not only of the Word become flesh but also of all those who live with his life (John 14:19ff.). She is, in other words, a figure of the church, the New Eve. This is the title the fathers of the church have given to her. In this role, we can see how relevant it is that she is again called "woman" in John 19:26. On Calvary, the beloved disciple, who stands for all Christians, is given to her to be her son and she to be his mother. By extension, she is given to all of us as well as our mother.

On Calvary we will see how the seeming rejection at Cana is clarified. Her intercessory power is effective only in virtue of the glorification of Christ. Nonetheless, even though that hour has not yet come, it is anticipated and her petition is granted. It is in the light of her role, therefore, that the reply of our Lord in verse 4 becomes consistent with his actions of verse 5 and what follows.

PURPOSE: Specific elements of Mary's life illuminate the church today.

SUMMARY: As the Second Vatican Council considered the nature of the church, it was able to find inspiration in Mary.

MUSINGS:

1. In the Foreword to this entire collection of Masses, Bishop Wilton D. Gregory has written a lovely reflection: "Throughout its history the Church has shown a special love and devotion to Mary. The Council of Ephesus bestowed upon the Blessed Virgin her highest and most significant title, *Theotokos*—'God-bearer,' that is, Mother of God. Century after century Mary has been praised as being 'higher than the cherubim and more glorious than the seraphim' because she said yes to God and through her the Word became flesh and lived among us."

2. "As the Church has reflected on the person and life of Mary, it has come to a deeper realization of what it is to follow Christ. In fact, the early Church saw her as the model—the ideal Christian—who faithfully follows the Lord in word and action. The Second Vatican Council referred to her as the Mother of the Church, since her cooperation in God's plan for the salvation of all helped to make the existence of the Church a reality in this world" (ibid.).

3. "Filled with the Holy Spirit, Mary cried out with joy that 'From this day all generations will call me blessed: the Almighty has done great things for me, and holy is his Name.' Mary's prophecy has become reality as the Church in the East and the West has glorified God for the humble virgin whom God has exalted for her ever-faithful love" (ibid.).

4. As we learn more about Mary we also learn a great deal more about salvation, faith, and the church.

RELATION TO THE EUCHARIST: "Do whatever he tells you" is an excellent motivation for the Eucharist.

Sources

Marian Reflections: The Angelus Messages of Pope John Paul II, ed. David O. Brown (Washington, NJ: AMI Press, 1990), 58, 62, 138, 139.
Lumen Gentium, chap. 8.
Guide for the Christian Assembly: A Background Book of the Mass, 9 vols., ed. Thierry Maertens and Jean Frisque (Notre Dame, IN: Fides Publishers, 1971), II:34; IV:251.

27. THE BLESSED VIRGIN MARY, IMAGE AND MOTHER OF THE CHURCH

III

Exegesis of the First Reading: Revelation 21:1-5a

I saw the new Jerusalem, as beautiful as a bride all dressed for her husband.

The book of Revelation is very complex and mysterious. It is filled throughout with images, illustrations, and allusions to truths, which are often difficult to fathom. Commentators, however, agreed that this passage is the high point of the book of Revelation. The last words of this passage are the only words spoken directly by the Lord in the whole book of Revelation.

This passage contains a number of images: a new creation, the sea, the holy city Jerusalem, a bride, a dwelling place, and a promise to end all suffering. All the images given here refer to or reflect a passage or image from another part of Scripture. Each image is to help us understand what Christ, Easter, and the church are all about. It is a new creation. The terrors of the sea are removed. Jerusalem, for the Jews, was and is the focal point of their worship, but now, we Christians have a new Jerusalem. The beauty and delight that a new bride radiates is the kind of beauty and delight we see in the resurrection.

"Behold, God's dwelling is with the human race" reflects the presence of God among his people in the garden with Adam and Eve, in the desert through forty years, and especially in the temple of Jerusalem. Now there is an even more intimate "presence" among us, God's presence in his church.

The point of the passage is that all these blessings are now extended to the new people of God.

Exegesis of the Gospel Reading: Luke 1:26-38

He will rule over the house of Jacob for ever.

The purpose of the Gospel of Luke and all the gospels is to announce the Good News. Saint Luke is unique in that he is never interested in details as such. He gives us many details but they are always to enhance the message. He is writing to alert his Jewish readers of the events, circumstances, prophecies, and persons with which they are already familiar. He is saying that in these events and persons, the hopes and expectations of the Hebrew people for the Messiah lay hidden. Luke's purpose is to reveal them. He tells us that they are all fulfilled in Jesus. Mary, the "favored one," plays an important role in this revelation. Symbolism abounds in this short passage. It is the second most frequently used passage in this entire collection of Masses.

Perhaps the most important symbol is that of the angel Gabriel, who had spoken to Daniel about the seventy weeks until the establishment of the kingdom (Dan 8:16; 9:21-24, 26). When the angel Gabriel tells Mary that the Holy Spirit will overshadow her, the angel reminds her, and all of us, that the "glory of the LORD filled the tabernacle" in the desert (Exod 40:35) and the Lord's glory had filled the temple (1 Kgs 8:11). When Mary raises a question about her virginity, some commentators suggest that she is concerned about the continence and virginity required in the Scriptures for those who would worship the Lord (Lev 5:16) or fight the Lord's battles (1 Sam 21:4). This may be the reason that this passage was chosen for this feast of Mary, image and model of the church.

Also in relation to her virginity, some commentators suggest that this is a literary device that allows Luke to remind us of what is required of the witnesses to the apostolic preaching upon which our faith rests.

PURPOSE: Once again, to see in Mary a model and example for the church to imitate.

SUMMARY: To see and hear with Christian eyes and ears allow us to see farther and hear things softer spoken.

MUSINGS:

1. The scene portrayed in these verses is very familiar to us. As we hear the words proclaimed, they are so familiar that we are able to say them along with the reader. This feast asks us to do more. We are to recognize in this scene the action of God toward us today, to us as church.

2. The Lord shows his love and regard for us by coming to us. The Lord reminds us that we have been redeemed by the death of his Son, and so we already enjoy the grace of salvation. Still more is expected of us. We are expected to be apostles to bring the Good News to the nations.

3. The image of Christ will inform us; the Holy Spirit will come upon us. Christ will be born in us. This is the plan the Father has for us. He awaits our response.

4. God had a plan for Mary. She responded. Now it is our turn. We must follow the example of Mary and from the depths of our hearts say with her, "May it be done to me according to your word." When that word is given, then all the images of the first reading spring forth in the church today.

5. Mary was the first to receive the Gospel. Mary was the first to evangelize.

RELATION TO THE EUCHARIST: Who is more worthy than Mary to show us and lead us on the way?

Sources

Do Whatever He Tells You: Reflections and Proposals for Promoting Marian Devotion (Rome: General Curia OSM, 1983), 26.
Guide for the Christian Assembly: A Background Book of the Mass, 9 vols., ed. Thierry Maertens and Jean Frisque (Notre Dame, IN: Fides Publishers, 1971), IV:162.
Ibid., I:142, IX:25, 90.

28. THE IMMACULATE HEART OF THE BLESSED VIRGIN MARY

Exegesis of the First Reading: Judith 13:17-20; 15:9

You are the highest honor of our race.

In this twenty-first century, we still recall with horror the horrible sufferings that the Jews in Europe suffered during the Holocaust, the Shoah. While we devoutly hope that it will be the last, it certainly was not the first time Jews suffered just for being Jews. The book of Judith tells the story of just such a crisis and how, through the instrumentality of this woman, Judith, the Hebrew people were delivered. Judith risked her life to save her people. God was her strength. The Jewish people, who were saved by her actions, then praised her for her sacrifice and courage. She is called "the glory of Jerusalem." As the Lord had delivered his people using Moses in the exodus story, so now, at the time of a new crisis of his people, the Lord delivers them through this woman, Judith. The Lord God is still the master.

Just a note about the expression "Lord God": if you check your Bible, you will find that in the Old Testament, "Lord" is often printed in small capitals—as it is in the Lectionary—indicating that this is the most holy name of God.

Although this book is not part of the Hebrew canon, parts of it were adopted by pious Jews as readings for their feast of Hanukkah.

Exegesis of the Gospel Reading: Luke 11:27-28

Blessed is the womb that bore you.

The Second Vatican Council used this passage of St. Luke when it spoke of the Blessed Virgin. Paragraph 58 of the Dogmatic Constitution on the Church (*Lumen Gentium*) reads, "In the public life of Jesus, Mary appears prominently; at the very beginning when at the marriage feast of Cana, moved with pity, she brought about by her intercession the beginning of miracles of Jesus the Messiah (see Jn 2:1-11)." In the course of her Son's preaching she received his praise. When he was explaining that his kingdom was more than the bonds of flesh and blood, he declared blessed those who heard and kept the word of God. This is exactly what she was doing most faithfully.

Jesus graciously accepted the praise offered to his mother by this woman and then elevated his mother beyond all other believers.

Exegesis of the Alternate Gospel Reading: Luke 2:46-51

The mother of Jesus treasured all these things in her heart.

Earlier in this chapter St. Luke used almost the same words as he described Mary. She "kept all these things, reflecting on them in her heart" (2:19). The first time was after the birth of Jesus and the visit of the angels and shepherds. Now, after she finds Jesus in the temple, we again have the expression, "[She] kept all these things in her heart."

This double reference to her heart and her silence presents Mary to us as a woman of wisdom who, in the light of the paschal event, re-members and keeps before herself the words and facts of the birth and infancy of her son. The booklet *Do Whatever He Tells You* tells us, "She questions herself about the meaning of obscure phrases. Overshadowed by the cross she accepts the silences of God with her own adoring si-lence. In silence, the heart of the Blessed Virgin appears as the ark in which the 'memories' of God's interventions in the history of Israel are conserved. It is the place where the times of 'before' are recalled. It is a place where reflections flow together and where the time 'after' begins. It is the earth in which the good seed has been sown and will bear much fruit. It is the coffer which will gradually be opened by the Spirit. It is a treasury which will enrich Mary and the Church. It is the ark, which holds the law of the Lord as light to guide our life."

PURPOSE: Who is more worthy than Mary to show us the way?

SUMMARY: As the book of Revelation points to the future of the church, it uses images that feature the example Mary gives us.

MUSINGS:

1. Judith was a good-looking woman. She used her natural talents to ingratiate herself with the king. In this way she was able to effect a change. Our natural talents, all our talents, have been given to us so that we may use them to do good.

2. The book of Judith is sometimes a violent book that describes violent times. We would make a mistake if we were to focus on the specific acts of violence and miss the larger messages that God continues to watch over his people.

3. The fact that the Shoah happened in the twentieth century reminds us that all evil has not been eliminated from this world even after the resurrection. We still need the intercession of the immaculate heart of Mary to change our hearts.

4. Devotion to the Sacred Heart of Jesus is widely spread throughout the church. The reason is clear. The symbol is so potent. When we want to illustrate the generous love of Christ for the elect, we look to his Sacred Heart and to Mary's.

5. Mary mirrors in her life and character the love and devotion of Jesus. In times of danger and crisis we can depend on Jesus, and likewise we can depend on Mary.

6. When we give ourselves to reflection, when we make a retreat, when we ponder the very same mysteries that filled Mary's life, we are like her. We do not need words; we need silence. John W. Lynch has written a book-length poem titled *A Woman Wrapped in Silence.*

7. Most importantly, like Mary we can, we must, listen to the word of God and keep it. Live it.

RELATION TO THE EUCHARIST: The fullness of the heart of Mary as she fulfilled her role as mother of the Savior is the model for us as we fulfill our role as disciples.

Sources

First Reading: *The Jerome Biblical Commentary*, ed. Raymond E. Brown, Joseph A. Fitzmyer, and Roland E. Murphy (Englewood Cliffs, NJ: Prentice-Hall, 1968).

Alternate Gospel: Do Whatever He Tells You: Reflections and Proposals for Promoting Marian Devotion (Rome: General Curia OSM, 1983), 58.

Guide for the Christian Assembly: A Background Book of the Mass, 9 vols., ed. Thierry Maertens and Jean Frisque (Notre Dame, IN: Fides Publishers, 1971), I:209; II:73; IX:14.

29. THE BLESSED VIRGIN MARY, QUEEN OF ALL CREATION

Exegesis of the First Reading: Isaiah 9:1-3, 5-6

The dominion of the Lord is boundless.

The Introduction to this collection of Masses tells us that the old and new covenant Scriptures form a single corpus that is permeated by the mystery of Christ. This principle is beautifully illustrated by the Scripture passages given for the present celebration.

Every time a new king was crowned in Israel, he was considered an adopted son of God and it was a cause for rejoicing. At the time of Isaiah, when the Babylonian armies were deporting the people, darkness was descending on Israel. It was the people of Israel who were walking in darkness. All seemed lost. Now Isaiah makes this announcement to stir up their hope. Literally this hope was vested in a future king who would throw off the yoke of oppression. Very soon, however, this pronouncement was turned into an eschatological event: the light of salvation in the person of the coming Messiah. No historical king of Judah ever realized this hope. They still wait in hope for the Messiah.

Christian tradition has always seen the fulfillment of this prophecy in Christ.

Exegesis of the Gospel Reading: Luke 1:26-38

You will conceive and bear a son.

As we read the Gospel of Luke we see that the details and style are generally symbolic and biblical. They open to us the mystery of redemption. This is not simply a story of early events in the life of Jesus. Every word, every allusion, allows a deeper insight into the mystery of salvation. Every verse reflects other portions of the Scriptures as mentioned before.

In this passage, the angel Gabriel draws on the prophets Zechariah and Zephaniah as he addresses the Virgin Mary. Zechariah (9:9) tells the daughter of Zion, the daughter of Jerusalem, to "[e]xult greatly." The Messiah would come to her, a "king," "a just savior," who would be meek and riding on an ass. Alluding to Zephaniah (3:6), who announced that the Messiah would come to Jerusalem, the angel tells Mary that the Messiah would come into her womb. The angel extends to Mary the privileges formerly attributed to Jerusalem. Zephaniah's influence is seen throughout the whole annunciation story.

Mary was full of grace, as was Ruth and Esther and the women described in Proverbs (Prov 5:19; 7:5; 18:22).

On a still deeper level, some see a matrimonial context in which Mary takes on the profound role as *spouse* of the Holy Spirit. God had been searching for a spouse who would be faithful to him. In Hosea (1:3), God repudiates his former spouse but is well disposed to a new betrothal. Thus we see that God is about to realize in Mary the mystery of all the promises by bringing about the mysterious union of two natures, divine and human, in the person of Jesus. Mary is indeed the Queen of the universe.

PURPOSE: This celebration allows us to expand on the celebration of Mary's assumption.

SUMMARY: As we meditate and reflect upon the gifts and blessings given to Mary, we naturally reflect on her present place in heaven and as Queen of heaven and all creation.

MUSINGS:

1. Saint Jerome gives us the same principle mentioned in the General Introduction about the use of the Scriptures. He put it more poetically: "The New Testament lies hidden in the Old and the Old is made manifest in the New." That principle comes to mind as we reflect on the Scripture passages chosen for this celebration.

2. The events that Isaiah portrays are eschatological events. They are coming—be ready.

3. For all the titles we give to the Blessed Virgin Mary and for all the pictures by which we depict her, we find a foundation in the Scriptures. First and most important of all, God chose her as Mother of the Lord Jesus.

4. The beginning of John's gospel says of Jesus, "He was in the beginning with God. All things came to be through him, and without him nothing came to be" (John 1:2-3). This is why we see him as the King of all creation and may quite properly speak of Mary as the Queen of creation.

5. The scene of the annunciation is the "acceptable time," the "day of salvation" (2 Cor 6:2). This is why the angel must use the words of the prophets to address the Mother of the Lord who is the King of creation. Again, this is why we may call her the "Queen of All Creation."

6. The most intimate of human relationships is that of husband and wife in the covenantal relationship of marriage. It is this intimate, special relationship that the commentary on the gospel is trying to draw upon. It is of the Holy Spirit that Mary is spouse.

7. Being Queen is not a question of crowns and regal trappings. Rather Jesus is King because in the Scriptures selected for this feast he is regarded as the Messiah and King, from the royal family of David. The prophets call on all to "[e]xult greatly" over the coming King. These words of the prophets include Mary, the Mother of the King.

RELATION TO THE EUCHARIST: We begin here on earth with our minds and hearts lifted to heaven and renewed, as we confidently approach the Eucharist.

Sources

Introduction to Collection of Masses of the Blessed Virgin Mary, 3.

Spouse: *The Jerome Biblical Commentary*, ed. Raymond E. Brown, Joseph A. Fitzmyer, and Roland E. Murphy (Englewood Cliffs, NJ: Prentice-Hall, 1968); Hosea 2:21.

Guide for the Christian Assembly: A Background Book of the Mass, 9 vols., ed. Thierry Maertens and Jean Frisque (Notre Dame, IN: Fides Publishers, 1971), I:142, 178; IX:25, 90.

SECTION 2

In this set of Masses, we address Mary as our helper in our spiritual development.

30. THE BLESSED VIRGIN MARY, MOTHER AND MEDIATRIX OF GRACE

Exegesis of the First Reading: Esther 8:3-8, 16-17a

How can I bear to see the evil that is to befall my people?

As we read this passage, we are met with a whole cast of characters about whom we know very little. The book of Esther is used only once during Lent in the daily Lectionary. The book tells a story of the Hebrew people, already being called Jews, while they were resident aliens in the Persian Empire. They were a minority, but they were very industrious. Some of the Jews of this story may have stayed in Persia after the time of the exile. The story is set when some very influential people of that country became jealous of the Jews and their accomplishments. These enemies, led by Haman, schemed to have all the Jews exterminated. This passage tells us of how Esther, whose uncle was Mordecai, appealed to the king and thwarted their evil plans and saved her people. They were helpless and hopeless, yet the Lord did not forget them.

The Jews celebrate this deliverance in their feast of Purim.

Exegesis of the Gospel Reading: John 2:1-11

The mother of Jesus said to him: They have no wine.

The Masses of this section describe the ways in which Mary helps us in the development and fostering of our spiritual lives. We can clearly see the motivation for choosing this gospel passage for the feast of Mary, Mother and Mediatrix of Grace. This is the fourth time we have used this passage from St. John, and it will be used five more times. We have already examined the background of this passage and its references to other parts of the Scriptures (see Mass nos. 9, 20, and 26). It is very important to examine the background of every passage of John's gospel since each contains subtle references to other parts of Scripture. John clarifies those passages and in return John's gospel is clarified by them. This scene gives us a picture of Mary in her solicitude, exquisite charity, and absolute faith.

Nothing is accidental in John's gospel. Because of that, we can infer that St. Joseph is dead since he is not mentioned.

PURPOSE: Mary at Cana exemplifies the power of Mary's intercession.

SUMMARY: Intercessory prayer, prayer when we are in need, is an important element in our relation to the Lord. This is illustrated by the example of Esther in the first covenant and Mary in the new.

MUSINGS:

1. When our Holy Father Bl. Pope John Paul II visited Ireland in 1979, he offered a special prayer to our Blessed Lady: "At this moment we listen with particular attention to your words: 'Do whatever my Son tells you.' And we wish to respond to your words with all our heart" (Homily at the Shrine of Our Lady of Knock). The Holy Father captures the meaning of Mary's mediation; it is our response to her Son Jesus.

2. The words that the Holy Father used in prayer may be understood as an instruction as well. He reminds us that our devotion to the Blessed Virgin Mary begins when she reminds us that we are to do whatever her Son tells us to do.

3. If we really try to do as Jesus says, then our hearts are transformed, our consciences are formed, and the words we speak all reflect the gospels. In return we can expect for ourselves the same solicitude Mary exercised toward the young couple at Cana. We can expect her to be our Mother and our Mediatrix.

4. Pope John Paul II reminds us that while the fathers of Vatican II hesitated to give Mary the title "Mediatrix," they did use it once in talking about her place in the church. They extolled Mary's mediating role from her consent to the angel's message to her motherhood in the order of grace.

5. The Holy Father reminds us that Vatican II asserted that her cooperation "in a wholly singular way" in the work of restoring supernatural life to souls in effect describes a Mediatrix.

RELATION TO THE EUCHARIST: We recall that Jesus said, "Do this in memory of me" and Mary said, "Do whatever he tells you," so both by Jesus and Mary, we are urged to celebrate the Eucharist.

Sources

The Jerome Biblical Commentary, ed. Raymond E. Brown, Joseph A. Fitzmyer, and Roland E. Murphy (Englewood Cliffs, NJ: Prentice-Hall, 1968).

Mediatrix: John Paul II, Council's Teaching on Mary, general audience (December 13, 1995).

Lumen Gentium 61.

Pope John Paul II, Homily at the Shrine of Our Lady of Knock, Ireland (September 30, 1979).

Pope John Paul II, *Redemptoris Mater* (Mother of the Redeemer), encyclical (March 25, 1987).

Guide for the Christian Assembly: A Background Book of the Mass, 9 vols., ed. Thierry Maertens and Jean Frisque (Notre Dame, IN: Fides Publishers, 1971), I:187.

31. THE BLESSED VIRGIN MARY, FOUNTAIN OF SALVATION

I

Exegesis of the First Reading: Ezekiel 47:1-2, 8-9, 12

I saw water flowing from the temple, and all who were touched by it were saved.

Ezekiel was both a priest in the temple and a prophet. He lived and prophesied after the exile. The people were rebuilding the new temple in Jerusalem and the times were hard. The people grumbled about their conditions. As a priest, Ezekiel was concerned about temple worship. On the other hand, in his role as a prophet he saw that his responsibility was to challenge the believers to greater and greater trust in the Lord. In this passage, Ezekiel, in a vision, sees the temple as the representation of the rock that Moses struck in the desert. The Hebrew people were suffering from the harshness of desert life, especially thirst. They began to quarrel among themselves and even with Moses. They grumbled against the Lord. In a dramatic response Moses struck the rock with his staff. As he did so, he exclaimed, "Is the LORD in our midst or not?" The water flowed. God was indeed in their midst.

Now it is as though Ezekiel transformed and transported that event to his own time and place and to the new temple they were building. He saw the temple as a representation of that rock. He sees, in his vision, water, which refreshed and restored the people in the desert, now coming from the temple to refresh and restore the people of his age. He wants to ask, as Moses did, "Is the LORD in our midst or not?" The waters flowed. God was indeed in their midst.

Exegesis of the Gospel Reading: John 19:25-37

One of the soldiers pierced his side with a lance,
and immediately there came out blood and water.

Every sentence of this passage, every word, is filled with meaning. We face many questions as we read this gospel. Are there three or four women at the cross? We never can figure that out. There is no doubt, however, that Mary, the mother of Jesus, was there even though St. John never uses her name anywhere in his gospel.

When Jesus speaks to his mother and to John, is Jesus concerned only for the physical care of Mary? Or is he making her the mother of us all? Is this the "hour" mentioned in John 2:4 and 13:1? This passage raises many questions. The very fact that it raises so many questions helps us to understand something of the depth of this gospel's meaning. We can hardly exhaust its fullness.

In the second section where Jesus is aware that "everything was now finished," John draws a parallel with the paschal lamb, which the Hebrew people were instructed to sacrifice when they were in slavery in Egypt. They were not to break its bones. The people then used the blood of the lamb to sign their doorposts so the Lord would pass over their homes (Exod 10).

As the soldier pierces the side of Jesus, blood and water flow down. John may not have been thinking of the sacraments of baptism and Eucharist, but certainly he was showing us symbolically, and sacramentally, that Jesus is the true Savior and Redeemer.

PURPOSE: To remind us that through the image of the fountain we have some notion of the grace that comes to us through Mary.

SUMMARY: Water from the temple was meant to renew and refresh the people of Israel. Water from the side of Christ renews and refreshes all humanity. And it comes from Mary.

MUSINGS:

1. To understand what the church is trying to teach us with the Scripture lessons of this feast, we must be familiar with the use of analogy. Analogy requires inference. From the things we know, we infer something we do not know. When Ezekiel sees water flowing from the temple in every direction, we infer that for us, it is Mary who, like a fountain, directs that flow.

2. In Eucharistic Prayer II, we pray, "You are indeed Holy, O Lord, the fount of all holiness." All grace and blessings come from God alone. Therefore, in the eucharistic prayer, the word "fountain" means the ultimate source. When we apply the word by analogy to Mary, we see her as the fountain of salvation.

3. A footnote in the Bible suggests that the great stream of water flowing from the temple is a symbolic restoration of fertility to barren ground. It is like a return to paradise. In the Near East, with water, it is a land of milk and honey; without it, it is a parched desert. Mary refreshes us on our journey.

4. The water supply came from rivers, cisterns, and, most beautifully, from fountains. So in our devotion to Mary, we hasten to her to receive through her gift the many graces her Son dispenses through her. We see her, therefore, as a Fountain of Salvation.

5. The gospel passage used in the first setting of this feast is read during the passion on Good Friday and again on the feast of the Sacred Heart. Its use on those occasions gives us a clue to its use here on this feast of Mary, Fountain of Salvation. The blood and water that flowed from his side are directed to us by and through Mary.

6. Here is a puzzle for you: Did Mary have two or three companions with her on Calvary? Scholars give different answers.

RELATION TO THE EUCHARIST: Refreshed and renewed by grace, we approach the source of all grace.

Sources

The Catholic Study Bible, ed. Donald Senior (New York: Oxford University Press, 1990), footnote to Ezek 47:1-12.

Guide for the Christian Assembly: A Background Book of the Mass, 9 vols., ed. Thierry Maertens and Jean Frisque (Notre Dame, IN: Fides Publishers, 1971), III:193, 334.

The Jerome Biblical Commentary, ed. Raymond E. Brown, Joseph A. Fitzmyer, and Roland E. Murphy (Englewood Cliffs, NJ: Prentice-Hall, 1968).

The Collegeville Bible Commentary, ed. Dianne Bergant and Robert J. Karris (Collegeville, MN: Liturgical Press, 1989).

II

Exegesis of the First Reading: Song of Songs 4:6-7, 9, 12-15

Fountain of the garden, well of living water.

The Song of Songs is, on the face of it, a love story that elevates human love above the superstitious practices of ancient religions. It is also seen as an analogy to the divine love, the love that God has for his people. Throughout the whole Song of Songs, the author uses images, forms, and symbols that may seem strange to us. He has already compared his beloved to doves, goats, and pomegranates. Now he speaks of her as though she were a garden herself that supplied choice fruits and pomegranates among them. The highest praise he could use to describe his beloved was to call her a fruitful garden with a fountain of fresh flowing water. The original audience was in the Near East where water was and is scarce. They would recognize better than most of us the special significance of a fountain in the garden. When the people had a reliable source of water—a running stream, cistern, or fountain—it was valued, protected, and cherished. It was the source of refreshment, abundance, and delight.

Exegesis of the Gospel Reading: John 7:37-39a

Streams of living water shall flow from his heart.

The imagery of flowing water found in the Song of Songs is found in this passage as well. Earlier in the gospel Jesus had spoken to the Samaritan woman at the well (John 4:7). He told her that he was the source of living water. The reason he would say this is because the Jews and the Samaritans of that time both spoke of the Torah as a stream that gave life. Now he takes up the theme again in this chapter. Those who believe in him would be filled with that living water, filled with the Spirit. He speaks of the faith required of all who would come to him. "Rivers of living water will flow from within him." It was this same Spirit that had overshadowed Mary. This is the origin of the image of a river from which graces flow.

PURPOSE: Grace not only refreshes and renews but it also delights.

SUMMARY: Moving from the image of a flowing stream to the image of a delightful, aromatic garden, we have a new insight into the grace that the Lord has bestowed on us through Mary.

MUSINGS:

1. Christian piety sees in the Song of Songs not only an expression of the love God has for his people but also an exchange between the Lord and the Blessed Virgin Mary. In this passage, it is as though the Lord were justifying his choice of Mary as the instrument of his graces. He praises her beauty, for she has ravished his heart.

2. Christian piety also sees the whole of the Song of Songs as an exchange between the Lord and the individual blessed soul. This prayer is expressed in meditation and contemplation.

3. Water is a fundamental image for all of us; it is so necessary for our lives. As mentioned above, the Jews and Samaritans spoke of the Torah as a stream of living water. The Qumran writings use the same image.

4. When St. John was composing his gospel, could he have been reflecting on the First Letter to the Corinthians where St. Paul speaks of drinking from the same spiritual rock, Christ (1 Cor 10:4)?

5. The Jews at the time of Jesus remembered the prophet Zechariah (14:8), where he says that Jerusalem is the source of all blessings. With this proclamation, Jesus is telling the world that things have changed. He, Jesus, is the source of living water.

RELATION TO THE EUCHARIST: Refreshed, renewed, and perfumed by grace, we approach the source of all grace.

Sources

The Jerome Biblical Commentary, ed. Raymond E. Brown, Joseph A. Fitzmyer, and
   Roland E. Murphy (Englewood Cliffs, NJ: Prentice-Hall, 1968).

The Collegeville Bible Commentary, ed. Dianne Bergant and Robert J. Karris (Collegeville, MN: Liturgical Press, 1989).

Guide for the Christian Assembly: A Background Book of the Mass, 9 vols., ed. Thierry
   Maertens and Jean Frisque (Notre Dame, IN: Fides Publishers, 1971), IV:294.

32. THE BLESSED VIRGIN MARY, MOTHER AND TEACHER IN THE SPIRIT

Exegesis of the First Reading: Proverbs 8:17-21, 34-35

Whoever finds me, finds life.

Historically, the Lord had instructed Israel through the priests, prophets, and kings. After the exile, the kings became entirely political. The priests became more and more concerned with temple worship and tended to be ritualistic and literalists and cut off from the life of the people. They would have been the antecedents to the Sadducees. Several reform groups began at this time as well. Daniel prayed to the Lord that the people no longer listened to the prophets (Dan 9:6). About the end of the fifth century BC, the Lord began to teach through wise men. These men knew from experience the importance of fidelity to the ancient traditions.

The whole work is delivered as though "Wisdom" were a person, a figure of speech where we attribute personal qualities to an abstraction. It is an attempt to make it more real.

This specific passage reminds us that the first condition of learning is the desire to learn, the love of learning. In that age as in ours, there was a tendency to measure God's blessing in material terms, in silver and gold. Here they and we remind ourselves that one who acquires wisdom had a treasure worth even more than silver or gold. Earlier in the book, the wise man spoke of the "fear of the LORD" as the "beginning of knowledge" (Prov 1:7). That is the theme of the entire book.

In the Roman Missal, this Book was known as the "book of Wisdom."

Exegesis of the Alternate First Reading: Isaiah 56:1, 6-7

My house will be called a house of prayer for all the peoples.

This is a startling passage. It opens up to strangers and outsiders the blessings of Israel. Many of the prophets had preached an exclusiveness that is at odds with this passage. In technical terms, it expresses a "universalism" in Israel as do the books of Ruth and Jonah. Now, everyone is welcome! There is a condition, of course: the observance of the law. Their behavior, offerings, and prayers will be acceptable to the Lord. They too will be brought to the holy mountain. They too will share with joy the house of the Lord. As Jesus himself will later affirm, this house will be a house of prayer for all the people (Mark 11:10).

Exegesis of the Gospel Reading: Matthew 12:46-50

Extending his hands toward the disciples, he said:
Here are my mother and my brothers.

We do not know the motivation of Jesus' mother and brethren in seeking Jesus at this time. It may very well be that they were even more aware of the hostility of the Pharisees against Jesus than Jesus was himself. They may have wanted to protect Jesus as best they could. They are here to show their concern.

We must remember, Matthew's gospel was written for the Jewish Christians at a time when the temple of Jerusalem had been destroyed and they were being expelled from the synagogues because of their belief in Christ. Temple membership had been a tie that had bound them together and now it was being torn apart.

There were still other questions to be answered. It was some time after the resurrection and the Christian community was being dispersed. How were they to continue to express their communion? Was it through ties with the members of Jesus' human family and his brethren who were still with them? Or was it rather through those upon whom the Spirit rested, namely, the apostles? All these elements enter into our understanding of this passage.

All those questions aside, the most important message here is how Jesus takes the concern of his mother and brethren to make a fundamental point about being a member of his family and discipleship in general. It is not who you know. It is not what you know. It is not the nobility of your family. It is how you respond to the Father's will.

Exegesis of the Alternate Gospel Reading: John 19:25-27

Woman, this is your son. This is your mother.

We have mentioned before that the best way to interpret the Scriptures is from the Scriptures themselves. The picture, which this gospel passage brings to our mind's eye, is the end of a story, not always the whole story. When we look carefully, we see it begins to take shape back in the desert of Sinai when Moses presented the covenant to the people and they responded, "Everything the LORD has said, we will do" (Exod 19:8). It included Mary's own beautiful response to the angel Gabriel: "Behold, I am the handmaid of the Lord / May it be done to me according to your word" (Luke 1:38). Essential also to the development of the picture is her role and her words at Cana: "Do whatever he tells you" (John 2:5). Together they weave the tapestry we see in our mind's eye, the scene on Calvary. Finally this is the hour.

PURPOSE: To find in Mary an example of prayer and contemplation.

SUMMARY: Scripture is a single whole; each passage contributes to the total mosaic. So from a variety of Scripture passages we develop a picture of Mary as model, mother, and teacher.

MUSINGS:

1. The very selections made for this feast itself contain a lesson. While none of the selections contain any of the words spoken by Mary, from them we learn a lesson from Mary, our Mother and teacher in the Spirit.

2. The style of the book of Proverbs is that of the personification of divine Wisdom. It is the revelation of God. Saints and Doctors of the Church throughout history have felt that portions of the book of Proverbs could appropriately be ascribed to Mary. "Those who love me, I also love, / and those who seek me find me" (Prov 8:17).

3. As noted in the exegesis of Isaiah, we find a note of universalism in the text. It is a very appropriate choice for this feast of Mary. She is Jewish. Muhammad accords her great respect in the Qur'an. She is the only woman named and indeed more is written in the Qur'an about Mary than is found in the New Testament. She is Mother of us all in the Spirit.

4. This gospel passage from St. Matthew teaches us a profound lesson about how radical Christianity is. Even today among devout Jews, the priestly cast of Aaron is still reverenced. Many Islamic leaders trace their relation and their authority to Muhammad. For Christians, however, Mary teaches us that our relationship to Christ is founded on faith. Only by faith are we related to the Lord. Faith, not family.

5. The words of Jesus in Matthew's gospel are, of course, a declaration of his mother's faith and will, but is it not also an invitation to all, women and men, to do the will of the Father?

6. The exchange on Calvary between Jesus, the beloved disciple, and Mary at this critical time could in no way be a simple filial concern. This is about all humankind. This observation has been made before and must be repeated here.

RELATION TO THE EUCHARIST: As brother, sister, and Mother, we approach the center of our faith.

Sources

The Jerome Biblical Commentary, ed. Raymond E. Brown, Joseph A. Fitzmyer, and Roland E. Murphy (Englewood Cliffs, NJ: Prentice-Hall, 1968).

The Collegeville Bible Commentary, ed. Dianne Bergant and Robert J. Karris (Collegeville, MN: Liturgical Press, 1989).

Guide for the Christian Assembly: A Background Book of the Mass, 9 vols., ed. Thierry Maertens and Jean Frisque (Notre Dame, IN: Fides Publishers, 1971), V:296; VI:195.

33. THE BLESSED VIRGIN MARY, MOTHER OF GOOD COUNSEL

Exegesis of the First Reading: Isaiah 9:1-3, 5-6

The Wonderful Counselor is given to us.

The General Introduction to this entire collection of Masses tells us that the old and new covenant Scriptures are a single body that is permeated by the mystery of Christ. This principle is beautifully illustrated by the Scripture passages used in this present celebration, passages that remind us of Christmas.

Every time a new king was crowned, he was considered an adopted son of God and it was a cause for rejoicing. At this time the Babylonian armies were deporting the people. Isaiah saw this, the beginning of the exile, as a darkness descending on Israel. They were like a people walking in darkness. All seemed lost. Nonetheless, Isaiah makes his announcement to bolster the hope of all Israel. Literally this hope was vested in a future king who would throw off the yoke of oppression. Very soon, however, this pronouncement was turned into an eschatological event where the light of salvation is the person of the Messiah. No historical king of Judah ever realized this hope.

Christian tradition has always seen in Christ the fulfillment of Isaiah's prophecy and at the same time, by analogy, we ascribe these blessed prophecies to Mary.

Exegesis of the Alternate First Reading: Acts 1:12-14; 2:1-4

*With one heart the disciples continued in steadfast prayer
with Mary, the mother of Jesus.*

Saint Luke has a preoccupation with Jerusalem. His gospel begins and ends in the temple of Jerusalem and with the Spirit. Now the disciples, under the guidance of the Spirit, will bring the gospel from Jerusalem to the ends of the earth. Before this happens, before the Holy Spirit comes upon them, the apostles, the disciples, and Mary, the mother of the Lord, are waiting together, in prayer. There is an eschatological dimension to their waiting, for they are waiting for the promised Holy Spirit. Watching and prayer should be the attitude of the new community of faith in the face of any decision they must make (see Acts 1:24-26; 4:24-30).

The Holy Spirit overshadowed Mary at the annunciation and now, as the Holy Spirit comes upon the disciples for their mission, Mary is there.

Exegesis of the Gospel Reading: John 2:1-11

The mother of Jesus said to the attendants: Do whatever he tells you.

The compilers of this section of the Mass collection had the intention of describing Mary's cooperation in fostering the spiritual life of the faithful. The unfolding of the story illustrates very clearly why this text was chosen for this feast of Mary, Mother of Good Counsel. We have already examined the background of this passage and its references to other parts of the Scriptures (see Mass nos. 9, 20, 26, and 30). It is very important to look back to examine the background of all passages of John's gospel since they contain subtle references to other parts of Scripture. Saint John clarifies them and in return is clarified by them.

Even without subtle references and competent scholarship we are aware of Mary's solicitude, exquisite charity, and absolute faith.

PURPOSE: We expect to receive good counsel from our mothers, and this is true for our spiritual Mother as well.

SUMMARY: Historically and instinctively, we Christian people have seen Mary as Mother of Good Counsel. As we read the Scriptures we see our intuitions are confirmed.

MUSINGS:

1. Often Bl. Pope John Paul II, in his *Angelus* messages, speaks of Mary as being in the lights and shadows of faith. He may very well have been reflecting on our first reading from Isaiah. The occasion may have been the birth of a king, but it was from his mother that the Wonder-Counselor came forth.

2. Consider the consternation of the couple, the family, and all the guests at the wedding in Cana as the wine failed. Mary did not wait to be asked. She initiated an action that led to the miraculous work of her Son.

3. "Do whatever he tells you." If Mary had never said another word, this expression would earn her the title "Mother of Good Counsel."

4. "Do whatever he tells you." Do we find in these words a vestige of the words of Exodus and Deuteronomy? When the Lord bestowed his covenant on the people, their response was, "Everything the LORD has said, we will do" (Exod 19:8; Deut 5:27).

5. Mary, more than the disciples, exemplified the very last verse of this reading. She recognized his glory and she believed in him.

6. The disciples, the women, and Mary were together in prayer—waiting. It is from Mary that they, and we, learn to wait for the coming of the Lord. She learned at Nazareth how to wait for the Holy Spirit and could give good counsel on how to do it.

RELATION TO THE EUCHARIST: Once again the command of the Lord and of Our Lady to do whatever he tells you leads us to the source of that command.

Sources

Marian Reflections: The Angelus Messages of Pope John Paul II, ed. David O. Brown (Washington, NJ: AMI Press, 1990).

Do Whatever He Tells You: Reflections and Proposals for Promoting Marian Devotion (Rome: General Curia OSM, 1983) 47, 76.

Servants of the *Magnificat*: The Canticle of the Blessed Virgin and Consecrated Life (Rome: General Curia OSM, 1996), 15, 20, 39, 92, 93.

Guide for the Christian Assembly: A Background Book of the Mass, 9 vols., ed. Thierry Maertens and Jean Frisque (Notre Dame, IN: Fides Publishers, 1971), II:73, 134, IV:251.

34. THE BLESSED VIRGIN MARY, CAUSE OF OUR JOY

Exegesis of the First Reading: Zechariah 2:14-17

Rejoice and be glad, Daughter of Zion.

The people of Jerusalem were still in the process of returning home from the exile when Zechariah uttered his prophecy. The city was full of confusion. There were so many things to do. Nonetheless, the people were joyful because they were returning home after years of exile. With a kind of holy exuberance Zechariah reverses the experience of trial and sorrow that they had been experiencing. He invites all to rejoice. When he says "all," it is a universal call; he is inviting even strangers, Gentiles, to join in the rejoicing.

We see two important developments in this passage. The first is the experience of joy after a time of trial. Second, there is the open invitation to "all" to share the joy. It was an important step forward for the Jewish people. It is one of the first hints of a universalism, of opening the message of salvation to people other than the Hebrew people.

When we hear the expression "the holy land," we know immediately what people are saying. It is interesting to note that here in Zechariah, we hear him use this term for the first time in the Scriptures.

How do we greet the Lord God? In silence.

Exegesis of the Alternate First Reading: Isaiah 61:9-11

I exult for joy in the Lord.

When Jesus began his public ministry in the synagogue of Nazareth, he quoted verses 1 and 2 of chapter 61 of Isaiah to announce the arrival of the Messiah. The whole poem in Isaiah had been composed to announce the joyful return to Jerusalem of the captives after the exile. The exile is over and we are coming home!

Isaiah gives us a number of images by which their joy was expressed:

It is like getting dressed for a celebration, with a whole new wardrobe.

It is like a bride on her wedding day.

It is like one wrapped in a "mantle of justice."

It is like spring with its beautiful flowers.

And what is the source of this joy? The blessing of the Lord God in returning the captives. The Lord is the source of all joy.

Exegesis of the Gospel Reading: Luke 1:39-47

As soon as Elizabeth heard Mary's greeting,
the infant leaped in her womb.

This passage was used for the feast of the Visitation on May 31st as well as in the Visitation of the Blessed Virgin Mary, Mass 3 in this collection.

In telling the story of Mary's visit to Elizabeth, St. Luke fills the story with allusions to Old Testament experiences. It reminds us of the stirring of the twin children of Rebecca while they were still in her womb (Gen 25:22). And of David's dance before the ark (2 Sam 6:16). Luke alludes to many other expressions of joy taken from the Psalms and prophets (Isa 35:6; Ps 114:6; Mal 3:20). His emphasis is on the expression of joy. It is more than the simple joy of friendship or kinship. It is the joy of salvation. The visit by the expectant Mary to the expectant Elizabeth is to bring joy and salvation both to Elizabeth and the child, John. And this is the cause of our joy.

Exegesis of the Alternate Gospel Reading: John 15:9-12

May my joy be within you.

At the Last Supper Jesus spoke to his disciples at great length. He had washed their feet, revealed the Father to them, and given them the new commandment. He promised them the Holy Spirit and told them of his plans for them. He had spoken of himself as the vine and of them as the branches. He told them of the suffering and hatred they would encounter in a hostile world. Finally, here Jesus becomes much more intimate, much more personal. He tells them of his love for them. Then Jesus gives them a guarantee. If they remain in his love and keep the command he had given them, they will in turn experience the gift of his love and the fullness of joy.

PURPOSE: As the title suggests, it is to show Mary as the cause of our joy.

SUMMARY: The ultimate cause of our joy is the salvation accomplished by the Lord. But the Lord uses Mary in her birth, life, and even death as the instrument by which the Lord showers that joy on his people.

MUSINGS:

1. The preface for this celebration included the expression that Mary is "the daughter of your love." This is a new and special way to consider Mary.

2. We are beginning the twenty-first century and our pace is frenetic. We flit from one activity to another. From lust to drink to greed, from fast cars, fast games, fast money. Part of the reason is the confusion between pleasure and joy. Pleasure is fleeting; joy is enduring.

3. Each of the readings of the celebration suggests, and the theme of the formula reflects, that it is the abiding presence of the Lord that is the true source of joy.

4. In both the readings from Zechariah and Isaiah we have the end of a story. Their stories began with the confusion, pain, and sorrow of the exile. The joy of the readings comes from the fact that now they are home!

5. The exegesis of the gospel suggests many Old Testament incidents to which St. Luke alludes and incorporates in his account of the visitation. Consider the words of King David when the ark was brought to him in Jerusalem: "How can the ark of the LORD come to me?" (2 Sam 6:9).

6. All of them are embraced in Mary's words: "My soul proclaims the greatness of the Lord; / my spirit rejoices in God my savior" (Luke 1:46-47).

7. Jesus at the Last Supper reminds us that his revelation and presence is the root cause of our complete joy. Mary was the instrument God sent to bring Jesus to us.

RELATION TO THE EUCHARIST: Let us go to the altar of God, the God who gave joy to our youth.

Sources

Holy Land: *The Jerome Biblical Commentary*, ed. Raymond E. Brown, Joseph A. Fitzmyer, and Roland E. Murphy (Englewood Cliffs, NJ: Prentice-Hall, 1968).

The Collegeville Bible Commentary, ed. Dianne Bergant and Robert J. Karris (Collegeville, MN: Liturgical Press, 1989).

Servants of the *Magnificat*: The Canticle of the Blessed Virgin and Consecrated Life (Rome: General Curia OSM, 1996), 75.

Do Whatever He Tells You: Reflections and Proposals for Promoting Marian Devotion (Rome: General Curia OSM, 1983), 34, 108.

Marian Reflections: The Angelus Messages of Pope John Paul II, ed. David O. Brown (Washington, NJ: AMI Press, 1990), 50.

Guide for the Christian Assembly: A Background Book of the Mass, 9 vols., ed. Thierry Maertens and Jean Frisque (Notre Dame, IN: Fides Publishers, 1971), I:91, 146; IV:203.

35. THE BLESSED VIRGIN MARY, PILLAR OF FAITH

Exegesis of the First Reading: Judith 13:14, 17-20

You have brought to nothing the enemies of your people.

The book of Judith is a story of God's loving providence for his people. It is not historical as we understand the term history. The story is told through the exploits of Judith. It is a captivating story and is a favorite subject for artists.

The situation as the author sets it up is that one of the cities of Israel is under siege. The people are in panic and ready to despair. Judith, a widow, has the courage to tell the city leaders that they should put their trust in the Lord; they should pray and offer sacrifices to the Lord. Judith does more than give advice. At the risk of her own life, Judith uses devious methods to enter the enemy camp. Then, using her wiles, she captivates the general. Later, when they are alone, she cuts off his head. This ends the threat to the Israelites.

As she returns to the city with the good news, Uzziah, one of the leaders, praises her with this beautiful prayer. She is an example, a heroine, a model, and a tower of strength to her people. She is a pillar of faith.

Exegesis of the Gospel Reading: Luke 11:27-28

Blessed is the womb that bore you!

Early in his gospel, St. Luke described Mary as one who thought long and hard about what she had heard. She was troubled by the greeting of the angel (Luke 1:29). A little later, she asked how the Lord would work his will (Luke 1:34). Later still, after the loss of Jesus in the temple, Luke told us that "his mother kept all these things in her heart" (Luke 2:51). Now, when a woman in the crowd raises her voice, we can see in this scene the completion and the fruit of Mary's reflections and meditations. Mary did more than listen. The words of her son and the work of the Spirit grew in her to deepen her faith.

We can never forget the words of St. Augustine that Mary was more blessed because she believed Jesus than for having been his mother.

PURPOSE: To see Mary as an example for our lives.

SUMMARY: In time of peril and crisis, it is a life of faith and utter confidence in the Lord, after the example of Judith, that will guide us through.

MUSINGS:

1. When we see the covenants, Old and New, are complementary, we will begin to look upon the whole body of books we call the Old Testament in a new light. Thus we should look at Judith as she appears in the whole book that bears her name. This short selection gives us only a partial picture.

2. The entrance antiphon for this Mass refers to the "pillar" of fire by which the Israelites were given to guide them in the desert. For us

it means that we put our trust in the Lord and not human prudence (Exod 13:21-22).

3. These lessons help to develop in us insights into the work of God in human affairs. From this story we can project our thoughts and devotions to insights into the place of Mary in our lives. We can use the words of Uzziah to honor Mary.

4. Judith was a widow, a holy woman, a religious woman. The book describes her as serving the Lord day and night. She was certain that salvation would come only through absolute fidelity to the Lord. She had no idea that she was to be the instrument of salvation. She simply was faithful to her service of the Lord. She was ready.

5. When God chose to use her to save his people in this critical situation, Uzziah will remind Judith that it is God calling on her service. In the story, the author describes her as being utterly alone at the time of her crisis. "[N]o one, small or great, was left." Her prayer at the time was, "Strengthen me this day, Lord, God of Israel!" (13:4, 7). She earned her triumph through prayer and observance.

6. Think of the debt of gratitude we owe to the anonymous woman of the gospel who gave Jesus the opportunity to give such praise to his mother. These were not the words of an angel; they were the words of Jesus himself.

RELATION TO THE EUCHARIST: As the Israelites had the pillar of fire to lead them in the desert and the strength of Judith's faith to strengthen them, so we have Mary.

Sources

The Jerome Biblical Commentary, ed. Raymond E. Brown, Joseph A. Fitzmyer, and Roland E. Murphy (Englewood Cliffs, NJ: Prentice-Hall, 1968).

The Collegeville Bible Commentary, ed. Dianne Bergant and Robert J. Karris (Collegeville, MN: Liturgical Press, 1989).

Servants of the *Magnificat*: The Canticle of the Blessed Virgin and Consecrated Life (Rome: General Curia OSM, 1996), 16.

Marian Reflections: The Angelus Messages of Pope John Paul II, ed. David O. Brown (Washington, NJ: AMI Press, 1990), 40, 54, 110.

Guide for the Christian Assembly: A Background Book of the Mass, 9 vols., ed. Thierry Maertens and Jean Frisque (Notre Dame, IN: Fides Publishers, 1971), VIII:148.

36. THE BLESSED VIRGIN MARY, MOTHER OF FAIREST LOVE

Exegesis of the First Reading: Sirach 24:17-21

I am the mother of fairest love.

The inspired author of this book lived in Jerusalem about 180 BC. He was very aware of the temple services and the law of Moses. His writings are important because he moves beyond just the words of the law to developing a spirit of dedication to the service of the Lord. He reminds us that what we know must show itself in action—that the profound truths of faith are not to be considered as "out there" but rather "right here." He reflects on the gifts the Lord had bestowed on his people and draws out some of the implications of those gifts. He uses the images of poetry to express his thoughts. We then extend them to Mary.

The book is not included in the Hebrew canon or in many Protestant editions of the Scriptures. In the 1950s the complete text was found written in Hebrew in a volume that predated Christianity. The literary form used in this book is personification, that is, the wisdom of the Lord is considered a person who speaks, reflects, and exhorts. Again, we extend his thoughts to Mary although the texts in the book refer properly to the wisdom of the Lord.

Exegesis of the Gospel Reading: Luke 1:26-38

Hail, full of grace.

Some Scripture scholars frequently examine the Scriptures verse by verse and word by word to exhaust their meaning. Other scholars study the Scriptures in a larger context where they are able to see directions and patterns that we might miss when we read verse by verse. These patterns, in turn, give us greater insights into the message, which the Scriptures wish to reveal.

Thus when these scholars examine the accounts of the birth of Jesus in the infancy narratives, they notice something very important. As St. Luke recounts the unfolding of the story of the birth of Jesus, the choices he makes of the Scripture quotations and the symbols he uses are remarkably similar to those used by St. John in his writings. Luke begins and ends his story in the temple. He mentions times, days, and weeks. These things are important in John's gospel as well. The most important fact is that Jesus is the promised Messiah.

In this passage, we must go all the way back to Abraham to understand its full significance. The Lord told Abraham that he, Abraham, was to be the father of a chosen race (Gen 12:1). The fulfillment of that promise would lie in the distant future. The people would have to wait and hope. In the meantime the Lord would watch over this people with his loving care. The Lord would hear their cries and lead them from the slavery of Egypt to the Promised Land. He would chastise them for their infidelities and allow them to be taken into exile. Again, God would lead them back from the exile. Through all these years, they continued to wait for the fullness of the Lord's promise. All this seems a long way from Luke's gospel, yet now, fifteen centuries later, the waiting is ended. When Mary says, "May it be done to me according to your word," the waiting is ended, the promise is fulfilled.

PURPOSE: To prepare a beautiful bouquet, we choose the finest flowers we can find and offer them to Our Lady.

SUMMARY: We understand the story of our redemption as an overall account from the fall of Adam and Eve to the Second Coming. Sirach and Mary are steps along the way.

MUSINGS:

1. As we read from the book of Sirach, we must be on our guard. The words, images, and poetry in this book sound very familiar, but they are used very differently. Very often in our society, these same words, images, poetry are used to debase human love. He uses them to extol pure love.

2. Beauty, taste, color, wonders, things that we see in nature and experience in our lives are meant here to elevate our thoughts and imagination. We are able to see through everything to honor the Lord.

3. How express the inexpressible? The author uses words, images, and poetry, as he attempts to give expression to the ineffable wisdom and providence of the Lord!

4. While the words of the book of Sirach are the words of the Lord, church fathers and spiritual writers over the centuries have appropriated them for Mary. The reason is clear: her constant association with Jesus the Word of God. We are in good company when we do the same.

5. What means does the gospel use to tell us about love? Again we find that it is a reversal of the secular order. When Mary says, "I am the handmaid of the Lord / May it be done to me according to your word," she is speaking words of love, obedience, faith, and responsibility. They are words of love, yet not the words ordinarily associated with love in our secular society. That alone should tell us something.

6. When Mary speaks her *fiat*, the whole history of God's loving care, God's providence, God's love for his people comes to a critical point. And more—that love of God is incarnated! What better illustration of Divine Love? Of fairest love?

RELATION TO THE EUCHARIST: We hear the invitation of the Lord himself as he calls, "Arise, my beloved, my beautiful one, and come!" (Responsorial Psalm).

Sources

Servants of the *Magnificat*: The Canticle of the Blessed Virgin and Consecrated Life (Rome: General Curia OSM, 1996), 65, 75, 79.

Lumen Gentium 56.

Marian Reflections: The Angelus Messages of Pope John Paul II, ed. David O. Brown (Washington, NJ: AMI Press, 1990), 91.

The Jerome Biblical Commentary, ed. Raymond E. Brown, Joseph A. Fitzmyer, and Roland E. Murphy (Englewood Cliffs, NJ: Prentice-Hall, 1968).

The Anchor Bible Dictionary, ed. David Noel Freedman et al. (New York: Doubleday, 1992).

Guide for the Christian Assembly: A Background Book of the Mass, 9 vols., ed. Thierry Maertens and Jean Frisque (Notre Dame, IN: Fides Publishers, 1971), I:142; IX:25, 90.

37. THE BLESSED VIRGIN MARY, MOTHER OF DIVINE HOPE

Exegesis of the First Reading: Sirach 24:9-12, 18-21

I am the mother of divine hope.

We find this passage from the book of Sirach just before the passage chosen for the Mass of the Blessed Virgin Mary, Mother of Fairest Love (no. 36). What was said there may be repeated here so we may place this passage in its proper context.

The overall message of the Scriptures beginning with the book of Genesis tells us of God's initiative toward his creation and of our human response. We have an account of how the Lord God called Abraham and how Abraham responded in faith. The Lord God promised Abraham that he would be the father of many nations but not immediately; the fulfillment of the promise would have to wait (Gen 17:4, 5).

Later the Lord God sent Moses to deliver his people from the slavery of Egypt; he had heard their cry. While they were in the desert, the Lord God gave Moses and all the Hebrew people the Ten Commandments, the sign of the covenant the Lord God had made with his people.

Subsequently, the history of God's people will bring them to the Promised Land, establish David as king; they will experience an exile and a return. Well over a thousand years had passed when Sirach was inspired by God to write this book. Sirach's purpose was to encourage people to keep up their faith in their religious heritage. Over those long years, they had grown slack. "Remember" and keep the law, he tells them. The law is the sign of the covenant with the Lord. Remember the Scriptures, he reminds them. The Scriptures show us the way to happiness. Remember your faith; it will sustain you, comfort you, and give you delight. It is the source of our hope. All this we ascribe to Mary as well.

Exegesis of the Gospel Reading: John 2:1-11

The mother of Jesus was at the wedding feast with him.

In the course of a careful reading of chapters 1 and 2 of John's gospel, we notice that St. John very carefully counted the days. He began with the eternity of God and then the incarnation. We see the expression "the next day" and again "the next day." The first verse of chapter 2 begins, "On the third day there was a wedding in Cana in Galilee." He has counted out seven days, the days of the old creation. With the marriage feast, John begins a new section of his gospel, beginning a new creation and the beginning of a new covenant. Nothing is accidental in John's gospel.

The focus of the account is the changing of water into wine. This is the first of several instances where John will look forward to and hope for the Eucharist. This is the first of Jesus' signs.

Mary, the mother of Jesus, figures prominently in this picture as well. Her role is more than just that of a concerned parent. Her position in the overall picture, painted by John from this point until he speaks of the woman in the book of Revelation (Rev 12), is one of a person actively involved in the unfolding of the message of salvation. She makes a request. It is denied. This reminds us that as important as Mary may be, Christ is first. The request is granted. Jesus anticipates his hour in response to his mother. He had not denigrated his mother. He reminds us of the priorities involved.

PURPOSE: To help us to open our eyes to the world around us and so raise our hopes.

SUMMARY: Generally we like to place our attention on the passages of Scripture chosen for a feast or celebration. Here, as in other celebrations, we have to look at the overall picture of salvation, not a single event but the event in the context of the whole.

MUSINGS:

1. On our way to an appointment, we will often look at our watch. We want to make sure we are on time. What the Scriptures do is make us forget our watches and look to eternity.

2. We should never be so narrow as to measure our lives in years. We are rooted in eternity.

3. The readings chosen for this celebration illustrate our hope. Sirach, as the exegesis suggests, is writing as much as fifteen hundred years after the first revelation. He reminds the people to keep hope alive.

4. When he speaks of God's law in such positive terms, he reminds his listeners to "remember." Remember how our ancestors hoped for the Messiah. He reminds them to strengthen their longing by their observance of the law.

5. In the letter to the Hebrews (11:1), the author defines faith as "the realization of what is hoped for and evidence of things not seen." The unity of faith and hope in this quotation is evident. It is evident also in our whole life of faith. We could just as easily say that our whole life is a life of hope. Our faith is like a light to light up the object of our hope.

6. Today the object of our memory is one of us, Mary, the mother of Jesus. She placed her trust, her hope in Jesus. He seemed to rebuff her. Ultimately, however, her trust was not misplaced. The response of

Jesus helped not just the couple at Cana; it pictured Mary as Mother of Divine Hope.

RELATION TO THE EUCHARIST: What better way to prepare for the Eucharist than to reflect seriously on the "first" of the signs of Jesus?

Sources

The Jerome Biblical Commentary, ed. Raymond E. Brown, Joseph A. Fitzmyer, and Roland E. Murphy (Englewood Cliffs, NJ: Prentice-Hall, 1968).

The Collegeville Bible Commentary, ed. Dianne Bergant and Robert J. Karris (Collegeville, MN: Liturgical Press, 1989).

Guide for the Christian Assembly: A Background Book of the Mass, 9 vols., ed. Thierry Maertens and Jean Frisque (Notre Dame, IN: Fides Publishers, 1971), I:142, 278; II:34.

38. HOLY MARY, MOTHER OF UNITY

Exegesis of the First Reading: Zephaniah 3:14-20

At the proper time I will gather you together.

This passage is so full of joy and happiness, of exultation and joy, that we might get the wrong impression of Zephaniah. He is first of all a prophet. His goals and purpose as prophet were to call Jerusalem back to careful observance of the law. He lived in Jerusalem and was active there sometime before the prophet Jeremiah. Jerusalem had lost its former fervor. It was a place of idolatry and sin. Zephaniah preached against this sinful condition. He prophesied dire consequences for Jerusalem.

As always, however, God never forgets his people. Zephaniah, in spite of his dire predictions earlier in the book, reminds the people that the Lord will visit and inhabit his city. The Lord will live with them. In this beautiful, joyful passage he reminds the people of the Lord's loving care personified in Jerusalem. It is the Lord who is the source of our joy and happiness. It is the Lord who gathers us together, who will bring us home and effect our restoration.

Exegesis of the Alternate First Reading: 1 Timothy 2:5-8

There is one mediator between God and humanity,
Christ Jesus, himself human.

The context of this passage is the insistence of St. Paul to Timothy that the prayer of the Christian must be universal. He had spoken of petitions, prayers, intercessions, and thanksgiving. These prayers are for everyone, even the governors and kings who at that time would have been pagan. Why pray for them? The fundamental reason is because there is one God. Because the salvation won by Jesus is universal and so must our prayers be. He amplifies this message here by reminding Timothy, and us, that Jesus is the one mediator between God and the human race. Our prayers, therefore, must exhibit solidarity with the human race in its concrete existence. Christ is the exemplar in all this.

Exegesis of the Gospel Reading: John 11:45-52

He will gather together in unity the scattered children of God.

This gospel passage refers to the miracle that Jesus performed in raising Lazarus from the dead. The miracle disturbed many people and aroused their curiosity. Many began to follow Jesus. For this reason some of them went to the Sanhedrin. They hoped that a word from the high priest Caiaphas against Jesus would condemn him to death and that his death would end the conversions to his way. Caiaphas may very well have spoken from a narrow nationalist view but it was, in spite of himself, a profound prophetic utterance. The death of Jesus will indeed result in the unity of all people. And Mary is his mother.

Exegesis of the Alternate Gospel Reading: John 17:20-26

May they be completely one.

Too often we do not take the time to read the whole of the Lord's discourse at the Last Supper. We know he spoke about love, washed the feet of his disciples, and prayed for unity. Too often, however, we know all this by secondhand.

We read this particular section of the Lord's discourse at the Last Supper late in the Easter season. As we listen to it here, it has the power to move us. As we listen to Jesus himself address his Father, we hear the hope that we all may be one in him as he is one with the Father. The unity of believers is based on the unity of Father and Son. Reciprocally, the unity of believers is to be a sign of the unity of Father and Son. It is a profoundly moving experience. This prayer seems to sum up the entire significance of Christ's life: that all may be one in him. This is the ultimate meaning of salvation. It is something we look forward to. We see also that there are two sources of unity, knowledge and love.

PURPOSE: We never see Mary alone. She is always with Jesus. This is why we see her with him in the work of bringing about unity.

SUMMARY: The intimate relationship between Jesus and Mary allows us to see the words of the Scriptures as reason to ascribe to Mary the insights of these Scriptures. What they say about the Lord may be said of Mary.

MUSINGS:

1. Even before the exile, the Hebrew people were badly divided. The exile tore them further apart. Now, as they return home, Jerusalem was the single goal for all of them. As Jerusalem was the sign of the presence of God among them, so it was likewise the source of unity.

2. It is the Lord who will bring the captives home to Jerusalem, who will bring about the restoration of Jerusalem, who will give them praise among all the nations. But, as we have learned before, we see the privileges of a Jerusalem restored bestowed on Mary. Mary, the Mother of Unity.

3. When preaching on Our Lady of Sorrows, Fr. Walter Burghardt, SJ, used this passage from Timothy. In the course of his reflections, he indicated that Mary's sorrows were shared with us very profoundly. This sharing of sorrow was indeed a source of profound unity.

4. Our union with Mary is part and parcel of our union in the Lord Jesus. It is from him that all other unions draw their strength.

5. We might repeat what we said about Caiaphas above. His words were spoken from a narrow nationalistic view, but they were, by God's revelation, a profound testimony to the unity of humankind in Christ.

6. How dare we listen to a conversation between the Son and the Father? Yet this is what we are doing in this gospel passage. He is talking about us to the Father! How much more appropriate are Jesus' words for his mother. The unity of which he speaks is personified in her. Where is our poetry when we need it?

RELATION TO THE EUCHARIST: The gospel uses the words of Jesus at that first Eucharist. What better preparation for our Eucharist?

Sources

Guide for the Christian Assembly: A Background Book of the Mass, 9 vols., ed. Thierry Maertens and Jean Frisque (Notre Dame, IN: Fides Publishers, 1971), I:92; III:246; IV:263; VII:85; VIII:54.

Walter J. Burghardt, *Christ in Ten Thousand Places: Homilies toward a New Millennium* (Mahwah, NJ: Paulist Press, 1999).

SECTION 3

The final subset of Masses reflects on Mary's role as intercessor for God's people.

39. HOLY MARY, QUEEN AND MOTHER OF MERCY

I

Exegesis of the First Reading: Esther C:12, 14-15, 25, 30

Queen Esther prays for her people.

The book of Esther was also used in the formula for Mary, Mother and Mediatrix of Grace (no. 30). The whole story of Esther is an exciting one. It is set in Persia at the time of the dispersion. At one point all the Jews were to suffer extermination at the hands of plotters who were jealous of their wealth. Esther was an orphan who had been raised by her devout uncle, Mordecai. There was only one chance that the people might be saved. Esther would have to enter the king's presence and plead for the people. There was danger in this. The law was that if anyone entered without being summoned, that person would be killed. Esther was very alone and very frightened. However, she had instructed her Uncle Mordecai to have all the people pray and fast. She would do the same herself to prepare for entrance into the king's presence and face her own death. This passage is part of her prayer. She recognized her weakness. She placed all her trust in the Lord's mercy. She took the chance to enter into the king's presence.

Her prayers were answered and the people were saved.

Exegesis of the Gospel Reading: John 2:1-11

The mother of Jesus was at the wedding feast with him.

This is a familiar passage and a familiar story. In our devotion we focus in a special way on the intercession of Mary. We are right in doing this since it is an important and pivotal development of the story of salvation. At the request of his mother, Jesus anticipates his hour.

There is much more involved here than just a caring neighbor's concern about the discomfort of friends at a wedding. It is the very beginning of the public life of Jesus. His newly recruited disciples are with him. This will be the first lesson he gives them.

Jesus had told Nathaniel (John 1:51) that they would see great signs. Thus when Jesus changes the water into wine, he is beginning to show those great signs to his disciples. Dare we say it was a decisive moment?

In the story, as St. John presents it, Mary has no hesitation. She sees a need and points it out to Jesus. The miracle Jesus then works is more than a gift to the embarrassed young couple; it is an introduction to faith for the apostles and the gift of a new covenant to us.

PURPOSE: Through the Scriptures we are able to establish a firm foundation for our devotion to Mary.

SUMMARY: If we know just a little more about Esther, we can better understand how dramatic her actions were. At the time no one could appear before the king without a royal summons. To do so meant immediate execution. Esther fortified herself with prayer and fasting and then entered the king's chamber. Her prayer was successful. She and all the Jewish people were spared.

MUSINGS:

1. With this celebration we begin the set of Masses that help us to see Mary in her role as compassionate intercessor for the faithful children of God.

2. The book of Esther has hardly ever been associated with Mary in our ordinary devotions to her. As it is used here, we have a perfect illustration of the goal of the compilers in developing this collection of Masses: from the example of Esther we see Mary in her role of intercessor as Esther was intercessor for her people.

3. Was Mary inspired by the story of Esther? She didn't have to say as Esther did, "I am taking my life in my hand," but she certainly, like Esther, took the initiative: she approached Jesus before his time.

4. The circumstances of Esther's life and those of Mary were as different as they can possibly be. Except in two things. Each was hesitant and afraid. Each put her entire trust in the Lord.

5. Saint John mentions the purification requirements of the old law to show that Jesus was now abrogating them. A new order is being established.

6. We should note also that the wedding feast is used in Hebrew Scriptures as a sign of the messianic age (Hos 2:21ff.; Jer 2:2; Isa 54:5ff.). Mary is present and has an active part in the transition.

7. The bishops at Vatican II said, "In the public life of Jesus, Mary appears prominently; at the very beginning when at the marriage feast of Cana, moved with pity, she brought about by her intercession the beginning of miracles of Jesus the Messiah (see Jn 2:1-11) (*Lumen Gentium* 58).

8. One of the first lessons Jesus taught his disciples was the power and influence of his mother.

RELATION TO THE EUCHARIST: Each of the Scripture selections tells of festal celebrations. What better preparation for the Eucharist?

Sources

The Jerome Biblical Commentary, ed. Raymond E. Brown, Joseph A. Fitzmyer, and Roland E. Murphy (Englewood Cliffs, NJ: Prentice-Hall, 1968).

The Collegeville Bible Commentary, ed. Dianne Bergant and Robert J. Karris (Collegeville, MN: Liturgical Press, 1989).

The New Dictionary of Theology, ed. J. A. Komonchak, M. Collins, and D. Lane (Collegeville, MN: Liturgical Press, 2000).

Guide for the Christian Assembly: A Background Book of the Mass, 9 vols., ed. Thierry Maertens and Jean Frisque (Notre Dame, IN: Fides Publishers, 1971), II:34.

II

Exegesis of the First Reading: Ephesians 2:4-10

God is rich in mercy.

When St. Paul was writing to the Ephesians, he understood that the world was in bad shape. It was torn apart. It was utterly bankrupt. God, who is rich in all things, has changed all that. Through Christ God has brought us all together, has risen from death, and has seated us in heaven. Put in simpler terms, God has given the free gift of salvation to us and now we examine both the immediate and the far-off consequences of this gift of God.

In even simpler terms, it has been suggested that what Paul here announces in precise theological terms is what Luke has set out in the story of the Prodigal Son (Luke 15) and what the church teaches in the feast of the Assumption. First there is our rich and merciful father who, even when we were dead because of our sins, still loves us. God himself brought us back to life through the death and rising of Christ. Even now he seats us with Christ at his right hand. God has bestowed on us the immeasurable riches of his grace.

This is the fascinating reflection that the scholars give us.

Exegesis of the Gospel Reading: Luke 1:39-55

The Lord has mercy on those who fear him in every generation.

We may not know for certain the date on which Paul's letter to the Ephesians was written nor the date of Luke's gospel, but we do know that each was recording the saving message of Jesus. We have St. Paul's account in our first reading. Here in the gospel, we have St. Luke delivering the very same message as Paul but as a story rather than as a thesis. Here we have characters and a specific situation, while the plot remains the same: the richness of the Lord's grace and the generous love he has for us. We find this same theme in the original message to Mary at the annunciation. Now it is continued in Mary's mission to spread the good news, first to Elizabeth. Without any merit on her part or on the part of Elizabeth or John, the grace of salvation is extended to them. The love of God encompasses them.

Mary's *Magnificat*, if we listen with a finely tuned ear, tells the same story once again. God is good and loving and merciful. God hears the cry of the poor and the downtrodden. The Lord offers his mercy from generation to generation. The Lord's treasures are given from age to age. The immeasurable wealth of mercy will extend to all who believe, forever.

PURPOSE: Each title and the Scriptures that accompany it have the purpose of showing us Mary in her role as advocate, as queen and mother.

SUMMARY: Through the words, deeds, and example of these heroic women of the Scriptures, we come to see and appreciate more deeply the generous gift of God's love for us.

MUSINGS:

1. The first reading, from Paul's letter to the Ephesians, moves us into serious theological territory. It is described in technical, theological terms, as both a realized and a future eschatology. He reminds us of the last days.

2. In the simplest terms eschatology means personal death, judgment, heaven or hell. We cannot confine ourselves to these simple terms, however, because St. Paul was talking about more than the individual. He was concerned with the destiny of the universe. Here we are concerned about Mary as Queen of that universe.

3. New teachers are given this advice: One, tell the students what you are going to teach them. Two, teach them. Three, then tell them what you have taught. Do we have the same situation here? Paul outlines the love of God for us. Luke then tells us the same truth in story form and he retells it three times: in the annunciation, in the visitation, and in Mary's *Magnificat*!

4. The chosen instrument to deliver the message of God's love for us is Mary.

5. Mary and Elizabeth, both with their unborn children, meet not just for a "girls' night out" but a profound reflection on what is happening—what has happened to them, what is about to happen. Their meeting was destiny!

RELATION TO THE EUCHARIST: The gospel uses the words of Jesus at that first Eucharist. What better preparation for our Eucharist?

Sources

The Jerome Biblical Commentary, ed. Raymond E. Brown, Joseph A. Fitzmyer, and Roland E. Murphy (Englewood Cliffs, NJ: Prentice-Hall, 1968).

The Collegeville Bible Commentary, ed. Dianne Bergant and Robert J. Karris (Collegeville, MN: Liturgical Press, 1989).

Guide for the Christian Assembly: A Background Book of the Mass, 9 vols., ed. Thierry Maertens and Jean Frisque (Notre Dame, IN: Fides Publishers, 1971), III:168; IX:65.

40. THE BLESSED VIRGIN MARY, MOTHER OF DIVINE PROVIDENCE

Exegesis of the First Reading: Isaiah 66:10-14

As a mother comforts her child, so I will comfort you.

The prophet Isaiah had been preaching to the people in Jerusalem. They would not listen. Earlier in this chapter, he had told them that the Lord rejects their temple sacrifices because they seemed to be empty. They were just words without meaning. The Lord was angry with his people and the prophet gave the Lord's anger a mighty voice. All this is found in the first nine verses of this chapter.

Now, the contrast is dramatic. He seems to be in an ecstasy of joy. All Jerusalem is to rejoice. The image he paints is of comfort, joy, contentment—a picture of intimacy. It is a picture of perfect peace. They were grateful not just for God's gifts but a superabundance of God's gifts.

Perhaps the most important expression is that the hearts of God's children will rejoice—their hearts! No longer will praise be only on their lips, something exterior, something superficial. No longer just words. Their hearts will change.

Exegesis of the Gospel Reading: John 2:1-11

The mother of Jesus was there. And his disciples believed in him.

The Dogmatic Constitution on the Church, *Lumen Gentium*, of Vatican II provides an excellent commentary on this passage when it links the feast of Cana with the events of Calvary:

> In the public life of Jesus, Mary appears prominently; at the very beginning when at the marriage feast of Cana, moved with pity, she brought about by her intercession the beginning of miracles of Jesus the Messiah (see Jn 2:1-11). In the course of her Son's preaching she accepted the words whereby, in extolling a kingdom beyond the concerns and ties of flesh and blood, he declared blessed those who heard and kept the word of God (see Mk 3:35; Lk 11:27-28) as she was faithfully doing (see Lk 2:19; 51). Thus the blessed Virgin advanced in her pilgrimage of

faith, and faithfully persevered in her union with her Son until she stood at the cross, in keeping with the divine plan (see Jn 19:25), suffering deeply with her only begotten Son, associating herself with his sacrifice in her mother's heart, and lovingly consenting to the immolation of this victim who was born of her. Finally, she was given by the same Christ Jesus dying on the cross as a mother to his disciple, with these words: "Woman, this is your Son" (Jn 19:26-27). (58)

PURPOSE: All the gifts of Providence are from the Lord but Mary is the Mother of the Lord!

SUMMARY: Isaiah tells of the sorrows of the exile, but he also shows the superabundance of blessings at the return.

MUSINGS:

1. An infant at the breast of its mother is a universal sign of peace, contentment, joy, and happiness. Our devotion to Mary is rewarded in the very same way. This is attested to by the innumerable images of Mary and the infant Jesus.

2. Mary's heart was the locus of both sorrow and joy. So the hearts of her children will likewise be the place of sorrow and, in today's feast, joy.

3. What is the source of Mary's powerful intercession? Why do we call on her confidently? Do we seem to go too far at times? From *Lumen Gentium* we read, "Mary's function as mother of humankind in no way obscures or diminishes this unique mediation of Christ, but rather shows its power" (60).

4. "All the Blessed Virgin's salutary influence on men and women originates not in any inner necessity but in the disposition of God" (ibid.).

5. "It flows forth from the superabundance of the merits of Christ, rests on his mediation, depends entirely on it and draws all its power from it. It does not hinder in any way the immediate union of the faithful with Christ" (ibid.).

6. And Mary was his mother.

RELATION TO THE EUCHARIST: The Lord has already blessed us with the abundance of his grace as he invites us to partake more fully.

Sources

The Jerome Biblical Commentary, ed. Raymond E. Brown, Joseph A. Fitzmyer, and Roland E. Murphy (Englewood Cliffs, NJ: Prentice-Hall, 1968).

The Collegeville Bible Commentary, ed. Dianne Bergant and Robert J. Karris (Collegeville, MN: Liturgical Press, 1989).

Marian Reflections: The Angelus Messages of Pope John Paul II, ed. David O. Brown (Washington, NJ: AMI Press, 1990), 58, 35.

Guide for the Christian Assembly: A Background Book of the Mass, 9 vols., ed. Thierry Maertens and Jean Frisque (Notre Dame, IN: Fides Publishers, 1971), II:34; V:142.

41. THE BLESSED VIRGIN MARY, MOTHER OF CONSOLATION

Exegesis of the First Reading: Isaiah 61:1-3, 10-11

The Spirit of the Lord sent me to comfort the brokenhearted.

As scholars read and reflect on the book of Isaiah, they detect a distinct shift of style and tone beginning with this chapter. The previous chapters of the book are filled with foreboding about the sins of the people and the coming doom and destruction of Jerusalem. Now, however, the tone is one of joy. Here and in the following chapters, there is rejoicing with songs and dancing.

In this section, the "Spirit" displays itself in these very external acts of joy. They are the songs of the Spirit's action among the people. The section is filled with metaphors of joy, how the children of God are released, are led into the light, and receive the glad tidings. It is like a new beginning.

Jesus used this passage to initiate his own public ministry, and we find echoes in Mary's *Magnificat*.

Exegesis of the Alternate First Reading: 2 Corinthians 1:3-7

God comforts us that we might comfort others in their sorrows.

The purpose of St. Paul in writing this Second Letter to the Corinthians is to address a number of problems that had arisen in the church.

Before he gets to his real purpose, however, he gives thanks to God for the gifts that we have all received in Christ. That is the key to the whole passage. It will likewise be the key to the solution of the difficulties in Corinth: in Christ! It is in Christ that we have received grace and salvation. It is our unity in Christ that is the source of these gifts, the source of the riches of God that we have received. It is the source of our knowledge of God and of God's word.

It is in Christ that we receive, as a free gift, the compassion of God and the encouragement from God in our every affliction. Because Christ suffered, his sufferings overflow to us, and through our union with him we take courage and consolation.

Exegesis of the Gospel Reading: Matthew 5:1-12

Blessed are those who mourn, for they shall be comforted.

This is the beginning of the Sermon on the Mount. Just before this, Jesus had chosen his disciples and now, on the mountain, he begins to announce to them the spirit of the new kingdom he is to initiate. Saint Matthew is writing to Christians who had been Jews. Moses, for them, was the great prophet. The Lord gave the commandments from Mount Sinai. Now Jesus, the Lord, from the mountain, gives us the new covenant. He details the nature of his new people. The blessed are the people who were called the *anawim*. They are people who have little or nothing. They have no worldly joy or comfort. In a sense, the poor, the meek, and those who mourn are very much alike. Later Jesus will tell his disciples that they are to offer no resistance to evil. Surprisingly, however, they are the ones whom the Lord Jesus calls blessed. They are the ones whose reward will be great in heaven.

Exegesis of the Alternate Gospel Reading: John 14:15-21, 25-27

I shall ask the Father, and the Father will give you another Advocate to be with you for ever.

The scene of this discourse is the Last Supper. Jesus has gathered his disciples for a final meal with them. As he speaks with them at length in chapters 13 to 17, he explains to them just what it means to be his disciple. Fundamentally, they are to love him and keep his commandments. In turn he will send an Advocate—the Holy Spirit will come upon them and remain in them.

This whole discourse is spoken with the realization of his imminent death. He has warned his disciples repeatedly that he is to be killed. Now he wants to reassure them that even when he leaves, he will not leave them alone. He will pray for them to have the Father send them another, the Paraclete. They will not be alone; they will never be alone. Rather there will be a new era marked by love. It will be an era also filled with the memory of Jesus and his gift of peace. These will be their comfort.

PURPOSE: More than any other person, Mary knows what it is to be a disciple of Jesus and, as such, a model of consolation.

SUMMARY: Mary is not mentioned in any of the Scripture selections. She does not have to be. She exemplifies all that Jesus says and does, all he invites us to be.

MUSINGS:

1. In modern America, and perhaps in most of the world, the most widely experienced pain is that of loneliness. There is the loneliness of the elderly, the loneliness of the alienated teenager, which figures so prominently in our news stories. There is sometimes even the loneliness of estranged partners in a marriage. Where does one find help?

2. Each of the readings applies directly to Jesus. Where is Mary? It is much more than a pious thought to say, where Jesus is, there is Mary.

3. As Jesus begins his public ministry, he will quote the words of the first reading. The very first message he brings to the world is comfort and healing.

4. The whole message of the incarnation seems to be summed up in the various Scripture passages chosen for this celebration. God is near. Christ, the Paraclete, and the Father are near. And Mary? Mary is likewise very near. She is near us. More than that, she is with us. She is never separated from her Son. She is always united with Jesus and with us.

5. For us the title "Mother of Consolation" is embodied in Mary. Our devotion to her is founded on her intimate and fundamental relationship with God. She said yes. She was there at the foot of the cross. In her deepest sorrows, she was ever close to God. She is the perfect illustration in herself of the comfort and consolation of God. As such, she can be for us the Mother of Consolation.

RELATION TO THE EUCHARIST: The Spirit of the Lord is also upon us as we prepare to celebrate the source of all consolation.

Sources

Guide for the Christian Assembly: A Background Book of the Mass, 9 vols., ed. Thierry Maertens and Jean Frisque (Notre Dame, IN: Fides Publishers, 1971), I:91; II:156; IV:201.

Servants of the *Magnificat*: The Canticle of the Blessed Virgin and Consecrated Life (Rome: General Curia OSM, 1996), 7.

42. THE BLESSED VIRGIN MARY, HELP OF CHRISTIANS

Exegesis of the First Reading: Revelation 12:1-3, 7-12ab, 17

A great sign appeared in the sky.

The book of Revelation throughout portrays the classic battle between good and evil. This was the theme of many pagan myths of the time. Saint John was writing to the churches of Asia, and the people there would have been familiar with those stories. The book of Revelation is so filled with such details that some scholars have suggested that John has taken something from every story he had ever heard and put it into his account.

All people of goodwill were waiting for a messiah to deliver them from the great evil of the age, generally identified with the Roman Empire. The empire for its part would brook no opposition. It was standing in wait to devour any possible opposition, any messiah. So there was a war in the heavens.

Jesus, the Messiah, had already ascended to heaven. He was out of the reach of the empire. The church was not, however. The church was persecuted. Believers gave their lives in defense of their faith. The church suffered.

Some people have suggested that the woman in this section might picture the Blessed Virgin Mary. This is very unlikely. Over the years we have used the details from this section to describe the Blessed Virgin; scholars have suggested that textual details are "ill-suited to such an explanation." This is not to diminish Mary but to remind us that true devotion to Mary is based on the solid foundation of an authentic interpretation of the Scriptures, not simply on picturesque words. So while the specific application of this passage may not have Mary in mind, it does, nonetheless, give us an insight into Mary's part in the ongoing struggle.

Exegesis of the Alternate First Reading: Genesis 3:1-6, 13-15

I will put enmity between you and the woman.

The word "myth" sometimes has a bad reputation. People tend to think that myth is fiction. Rather, it is the opposite. Myths, as in this story, tell us in dramatic form things that are very profound and so very true. We Christians look on Jesus as our Redeemer and Messiah. He is the one who has forgiven our sins and made us truly children of God. It is this story of the sin of Adam and Eve that tells us why we needed a redeemer, a messiah, in the first place. That is the point of the story and it is profoundly true.

As the *Catechism of the Catholic Church* puts it, "The account of the fall in *Genesis* 3 uses figurative language but affirms a primeval event, a deed that took place *at the beginning of the history of man.*† Revelation gives us the certainty of faith that the whole of human history is marked by the original fault freely committed by our first parents"†† (390).

Scholars suggest that the very words in the mouth of Satan were a distortion of God's intention. Eve further distorted God's intention. Sin begins with a lie and with a choice to set one's self against God. This very familiar story has profound theological meaning.

Exegesis of the Gospel Reading: John 2:1-11

This was the first of Jesus' signs.

As always, when we have a passage from John's gospel we find that it is overflowing with meaning. Saint John was writing seventy years after the events he records. He has had time to reflect on the deep significance of the events that he and the other disciples may have missed at the time they experienced them. In this passage, he is careful to count the days and to record the hours. This story is so vivid that it seems to have been an eyewitness account.

---

† Here the Catechism includes the following note: "Cf. *Gaudium et spes* 13§1."

†† "Cf. Council of Trent: Denziger-Schönmetzer, *Enchiridion Symbolorum, definitionum et declarationum de rebus fidei et morum* (1965) 1513; Pius XII: Denziger-Schönmetzer 3897; Paul VI: *Acta Apostolicae Sedis* 58 (1966), 654."

The first verse of this chapter reads, "On the third day there was a wedding" that was three days after speaking with Nathanael. As John carefully counted the days since Jesus was baptized in the Jordan, this is the seventh day. Now is the time for a new creation, a new creation story, and a turning point in the history of salvation.

It is clear that Mary was more than just a guest at the wedding. Her part was something official. She had the authority to give orders to the servants. When there was trouble, however, she turned to Jesus for help.

After her appeal to Jesus, three strange things happened. First he addressed her, his own mother, as "Woman." Jesus will again address Mary as "Woman" when he is hanging on the cross. From her actions we know that she did not consider this form of address as any kind of affront, strange as it may sound to us.

The second strange thing is that Jesus seemed to refuse her. Neither did this bother her. It is almost as though he said, why did you even have to ask? She did not hesitate. She instructed the servants to obey him; they were to do whatever he tells them.

The third unusual thing is the amount of wine that Jesus provided for the wedding. It came out to well over 180 gallons of wine. God is generous in response to his Mother.

PURPOSE: Mary is our help in time of trial and conflict.

SUMMARY: Creation itself is a gift, as is revelation and, the greatest gift of all, the incarnation. God chose Mary to effect the incarnation and so she is quite truly the help of Christians.

MUSINGS:

1. Conflict seems constant in our human condition. All the Scripture selections for this formula seem to feature conflict in one way or another.

2. Image is very important to our devotional life. Even theologians agree to this while they suggest that this image is not of Mary. In the opening reading we have a wonderful image, and the church chooses to use it to honor Mary.

3. We might consider the book of Revelation as something of a mirror. It pictures the violent clash between good and evil on a cosmic scale. The whole of the heavens is involved. It is a mirror, however, because we see a similar struggle in almost every soul. For some it seems that the same titanic struggle takes place within one's soul.

4. The book of Genesis reminds us that sin entered this world by the free choice of the gift over the Giver. We all have that wonderful, yet tragic, gift of free will. As we reflect, we see that all too often we ourselves are the root cause of the conflicts we experience.

5. At Cana, the difficulty with the shortage of wine was trivial compared with the momentous difficulties we experience personally and/or collectively in the world today. The solution, however, is the same. Bring the difficulty to Mary.

6. One hundred eighty gallons of wine! What a party! Yet the story is not just about wine and the wedding feast. It is about the beginning of a new covenant and the superabundant graces the Lord gives us: "and his disciples began to believe in him."

7. In the desert when Moses gave the commandments to the Hebrew people, they said in unison, Whatever the Lord asks of us, we will do. We find in Mary's instructions to the servants an echo of that response. No wonder she is invoked as Help of Christians.

RELATION TO THE EUCHARIST: The command of Mary to the servants at Cana is an invitation to us to do likewise, that is, to do whatever he tells us.

Sources

The Jerome Biblical Commentary, ed. Raymond E. Brown, Joseph A. Fitzmyer, and Roland E. Murphy (Englewood Cliffs, NJ: Prentice-Hall, 1968).

The Collegeville Bible Commentary, ed. Dianne Bergant and Robert J. Karris (Collegeville, MN: Liturgical Press, 1989).

Do Whatever He Tells You: Reflections and Proposals for Promoting Marian Devotion (Rome: General Curia OSM, 1983), 69.

Guide for the Christian Assembly: A Background Book of the Mass, 9 vols., ed. Thierry Maertens and Jean Frisque (Notre Dame, IN: Fides Publishers, 1971), II:223, 34.

43. OUR LADY OF RANSOM

Exegesis of the First Reading: Judith 15:8-10; 16:13-14

The hand of the Lord strengthened me.

This story of Judith is set when Nebuchadnezzar was king of Babylon. King Nebuchadnezzar had sent his armies to conquer Palestine and Jerusalem. The army surrounded Jerusalem and the city was being heavily besieged. In a very heroic action, full of danger to herself, Judith killed the army commander and Jerusalem was saved.

The words of the high priest Joakim were spoken in thanksgiving for the blessing of their ransom. Long before the coming of the Messiah, these words are a beautiful expression of gratitude to the Lord. They received the gift through the actions of Judith, and so she is properly praised. The words tell of the joy of salvation.

Judith also prayed a prayer of thanksgiving, attributing all her works to the Lord. The people were in mortal danger, and through the inspiration, courage, and initiation of this woman, they were saved. They were grateful. This is the message.

Exegesis of the Gospel Reading: John 19:25-27

Woman, this is your son.

The silhouetted cross and figures standing beneath it stamp an indelible mark in our minds. It is so familiar a scene in Christian devotion that we can never forget it. As familiar as it seems, however, we can still gain new insights into the wealth of what is taking place by changing our perspective. Think of it as an annunciation, a cross annunciation.

There is a big picture: The Lord of all creation hangs on the cross as a sign to all creation of the love he has for his creatures. God's love for us was the motive of the incarnation of his Son. God's love for us was the motivation for the crucifixion of Jesus. That love was announced in the story of the annunciation and it was announced again on Calvary.

Then there is the smaller picture. In the midst of his pain and suffering for all creation, Jesus has concern for each of us, and, specifically, his mother. The way he had addressed her at Cana at the beginning of his public ministry is the way he addresses her now at its end. At Cana he initiated his public life, and his disciples believed in him. Here, however, all those disciples, John excepted, have abandoned him. It is to John, the faithful one, he entrusts his mother. John, representing each of us, accepts her into his home.

PURPOSE: So often in times of trial, persecution, or sickness, we feel powerless. Mary helps us in our weakness; she ransoms us.

SUMMARY: On God's promise we are never alone, never helpless. As God has created us, so he assists us through Mary.

MUSINGS:

1. In our mind's eye, can we transpose the scene from the book of Judith to the hill country of Judah, to the home of Elizabeth and Zechariah, and to the meeting of Mary and Elizabeth? Doesn't Elizabeth echo the words of the high priest when she says to Mary, "May you be blessed by the LORD Almighty forever and ever!"

2. May we likewise hear in the words of Mary's *Magnificat* an echo of the words of Judith herself?

3. *Lumen Gentium* 58 tells us, "Thus the blessed Virgin advanced in her pilgrimage of faith, and faithfully persevered in her union with her Son until she stood at the cross, in keeping with the divine plan (see Jn 19:25), suffering deeply with her only begotten Son, associating herself with his sacrifice in her mother's heart, and lovingly consenting to the immolation of this victim who was born of her. Finally, she was given by the same Christ Jesus dying on the cross as a mother to his disciple, with these words: 'Woman, this is your Son' (Jn 19:26-27)."

4. The gospel is really like a diamond. It is precious. But, more important, it has multiple facets. From whatever angle we view it, it presents us with a special luster. So we may ask, who was more favored?

5. Or dare we speak of the exchange on Calvary as a "cross annunciation"? As the Lord God bestowed his love upon us in the joyful circumstances of Nazareth, now as he shares in a special way the pain and sufferings of human kind, he announces once again his undying love. Mary is there, cooperating with God once again.

RELATION TO THE EUCHARIST: In our weakness we need help. Where do we go to find it? Where else than to the Eucharist?

Sources

Ambrose Mayer, OSM, *The Cross Annunciation* (Portland: Sanctuary of Our Lady of Sorrows, 1931).

Servants of the *Magnificat:* The Canticle of the Blessed Virgin and Consecrated Life (Rome: General Curia OSM, 1996), 92.

The Jerome Biblical Commentary, ed. Raymond E. Brown, Joseph A. Fitzmyer, and Roland E. Murphy (Englewood Cliffs, NJ: Prentice-Hall, 1968).

The Collegeville Bible Commentary, ed. Dianne Bergant and Robert J. Karris (Collegeville, MN: Liturgical Press, 1989).

Guide for the Christian Assembly: A Background Book of the Mass, 9 vols., ed. Thierry Maertens and Jean Frisque (Notre Dame, IN: Fides Publishers, 1971), IX:65.

44. THE BLESSED VIRGIN MARY, HEALTH OF THE SICK

Exegesis of the First Reading: Isaiah 53:1-5, 7-10

He bore our sufferings himself.

There is no question that human suffering offers a tremendous challenge to us. Over the years many theologians have offered their solutions, some better than others. By choosing this passage, the authors seem to want us to see the solidarity of the human family so that when something happens to one of us, it happens to all of us. In this passage, Isaiah sees the suffering, of which he speaks, as the suffering for all people in all history. He includes the suffering that the people had experienced in Egypt as well as the sufferings of Jeremiah and his own suffering. We Christians see in Isaiah a prototype of Christ who took upon himself the sins and all the sufferings of all people everywhere and for all time. In himself he is guiltless, but he accepts the sufferings on behalf of all.

Exegesis of the Gospel Reading: Luke 1:39-56

Why should I be honored with a visit from the mother of my Lord?

As we consider the context of this scene, perhaps the very first thing we should notice is that no men are present.

Second, we remember that Mary just had a visit from the angel who addressed her as one who enjoyed God's favor and told her that the

Lord was with her and the Holy Spirit would come upon her. In a word, God chose her. Then, by her *fiat* she gave her consent to this election. What is the next thing she does?

She sets out upon her mission with haste. In commenting on this story of the visitation, some authors have suggested that we might properly see this meeting as the very first Pentecost. The gospel says that Elizabeth, at the sound of Mary's voice, was "filled with the holy Spirit." Elizabeth then gave us the words that we still use to address Mary: "blessed are you among women." In a previous Mass formula (no. 43) we noted how Judith had been blessed for her work on behalf of the people, and now Elizabeth blesses Mary for the mission she has undertaken.

Mary then begins her second mission, a mission to all people. She gives expression to this mission with her *Magnificat*.

The *Magnificat* is first of all a song, which is filled with mercy, joy, and hope. It overflows with gratitude, holiness, blessedness, and wonder at God's works. These sentiments just begin to touch the depths to be found in this prayer, and in it also we find a plan for social justice.

PURPOSE: Redemption is total, body and soul. Jesus uses Mary as his instrument for healing.

SUMMARY: The point of the incarnation is that Jesus shares with us all that is human, even weakness and illness. He likewise shares comfort and healing.

MUSINGS:

1. We must remind ourselves that the decree that established this collection taught us that all Scripture is a single corpus, the best interpretation of Scripture is Scripture itself, and we will find in these passages illustrations of the virtues we find in Mary, the first and most perfect disciple of Christ.

2. We don't have to refer to a recent tragedy to ask why there is suffering in the world. The question has been asked all through history. Why? Apart from God, it is meaningless. Early in the Old Testament, suffering was always a punishment for sin. After the exile, fidelity in the midst of suffering was seen as a light to the world.

3. In Isaiah, we see suffering in a new way. The Servant of the Lord would take upon himself the sufferings of others. In this passage, Christians have traditionally seen an image of Christ who takes our sins and our sufferings to himself.

4. There are no men in this gospel passage, but still in the exchange of these two women we have the affirmation of the incarnation and salvation.

5. As suggested in the exegesis, some see this visit as the first Pentecost. Mary is the first to bring us words of comfort and solace. May we also see her as an instrument of the Spirit?

6. Mary's great prayer is the prayer of a prophet. Like a prophet, Mary speaks of God's works, recalls God's saving deeds, and remembers the promises made to the Father. She examines the present and looks ahead to the future. It is she who speaks the first prophetic utterance of the new covenant. It is she who is the health of the sick.

RELATION TO THE EUCHARIST: As we celebrate the Eucharist we are celebrating the source of all our well-being.

Sources

Richard Sparks, CSP, "Suffering," in *The New Dictionary of Catholic Spirituality*, ed. Michael Downey (Collegeville, MN: Liturgical Press, 2000).

Servants of the *Magnificat*: The Canticle of the Blessed Virgin and Consecrated Life (Rome: General Curia OSM, 1996), 85.

The Anchor Bible Dictionary, ed. David Noel Freedman et al. (New York: Doubleday, 1992).

Guide for the Christian Assembly: A Background Book of the Mass, 9 vols., ed. Thierry Maertens and Jean Frisque (Notre Dame, IN: Fides Publishers, 1971), III:293; IX:65.

45. THE BLESSED VIRGIN MARY, QUEEN OF PEACE

Exegesis of the First Reading: Isaiah 9:1-3, 5-6

The dominion of the Lord is boundless in a peace that has no end.

The Assyrian armies had conquered the land and every day more and more people were taken away into captivity. These were terrible times for Israel. Some of the captives were blinded and destined to live in darkness. But, says the prophet, those who walk in darkness will see a great light. There will be a savior, a redeemer. They will be freed from evil and participate in the joys of the Messiah. The reaffirmation of the eternal covenant, and the hope that would accompany this reaffirmation, will come through a child. The light will come through this child, a king, who is of the line of David and endowed with all the virtues of King David. He will be the Prince of Peace.

We, of course, see the fulfillment of this hope in Christ, the son of Mary.

Exegesis of the Gospel Reading: Luke 1:26-38

You will conceive and bear a son.

The angel greeted Mary with words from the prophets Zephaniah and Zechariah. Zephaniah said, "Do not fear, Zion, do not be discouraged!" (Zeph 3:16). It was the prophet Zechariah who said, "Exult greatly, O daughter Zion! / Shout for joy, O daughter Jerusalem!" (Zech 9:9). The prophets used these words when they saluted Jerusalem as the source of the coming Messiah. The angel now transfers these titles to Mary and so reminds us that it is from her, Mary, that the Messiah will come.

For St. Luke, Jerusalem is the source and center of faith. His gospel leads Jesus to Jerusalem and then, in the Acts of the Apostles, he shows how the faith spreads from Jerusalem to the whole world.

The fathers of the church taught that this special, solemn, and beautiful greeting offered to Mary showed that all the divine graces reposed in the Mother of God and that she was adorned with all the gifts of the Holy Spirit. Her questions and apprehension did not arise from any lack of faith. Rather, they served to help us realize that she was a knowing and willing cooperator in the divine plan.

Once she learns of the implications of God's plan for her, Mary gives her unwavering assent: "Behold, I am the handmaid of the Lord. / May it be done to me according to your word."

PURPOSE: God's promise of peace given through Isaiah was accomplished through Mary.

SUMMARY: All Scripture is a single body, so as we read Isaiah about a future peace giver we hear him speaking of Jesus the son of Mary.

MUSINGS:

1. We might characterize much Old Testament writing through the saying, "On the one hand and on the other." So, here in Isaiah, we have a very dramatic portrayal of the conflict of good and evil, a conflict between light and dark, suffering and joy.

2. More important is the contrast Isaiah made between war and peace. Isaiah was speaking of the trials and tribulations brought about by the war that Assyria was waging against Israel. What he said about that particular war we may extend to every war.

3. However, at the very same time, when things seemed to be at their worst, still there was hope.

4. The principle images of Isaiah are light and new birth. We see the complete fulfillment of the prophecies in Jesus. He is the Prince of Peace.

5. In the book of Genesis we read that "Abram went as the LORD directed him" (12:4). This was the first act of faith. It is the reason why we call Abraham our father in faith. We believe that the words of Mary are not less momentous. The words of Abraham spoken in Genesis mark the beginning of the life of faith; Mary marks its continuation.

6. The words spoken by Mary mark the beginning of a new life of grace in Christ, the Prince of Peace.

7. The instrument that God used to effect his plan: Mary, Queen of Peace.

RELATION TO THE EUCHARIST: We celebrate the Eucharist with profound gratitude for the gifts the Lord has given us, among them the gift of peace.

Sources

Guide for the Christian Assembly: A Background Book of the Mass, 9 vols., ed. Thierry Maertens and Jean Frisque (Notre Dame, IN: Fides Publishers, 1971), I:173; II:73. Ibid., I:142; IX:25, 90.

The Jerome Biblical Commentary, ed. Raymond E. Brown, Joseph A. Fitzmyer, and Roland E. Murphy (Englewood Cliffs, NJ: Prentice-Hall, 1968).

The Collegeville Bible Commentary, ed. Dianne Bergant and Robert J. Karris (Collegeville, MN: Liturgical Press, 1989).

46. THE BLESSED VIRGIN MARY, GATE OF HEAVEN

Exegesis of the First Reading: Revelation 21:1-5a

I saw the new Jerusalem, as beautiful as a bride
all dressed for her husband.

As we read the book of Revelation the images that the author uses reflect the whole Jewish heritage. We must remember also that at this time the majority of the followers of Christ were Jewish. However, by the time the book of Revelation was inspired, Jerusalem had been destroyed. The events the author records reflect both this Jewish heritage and the crises of the times. The images of this passage are taken from Jeremiah and Isaiah (Jer 31:35; Isa 27:1; 65:17; 66:12ff.). Isaiah especially spoke of how Jerusalem would be forgotten but would be rebuilt. The book of Revelation takes us in a radically new direction. There is a new Jerusalem, one that transcends the earthly Jerusalem, a new Jerusalem already completely rebuilt, adorned as a bride for her husband.

This new Jerusalem is "coming down" now. It is not something only for a distant future. Those who were baptized may have looked forward to heaven, but they also believed in the reality of God's presence here on earth, right here, right now. It is a very special dwelling place. It is God's dwelling place with the human race. The author is telling us here what the book of Kings told us about the temple of Solomon: "the glory of the LORD" filled that temple (1 Kgs 8:10-11).

The joy will be like the joy of the captives returning from exile. There will be no more tears, no more death nor mourning. There is a new order.

In the last verse, it is the Lord God who speaks—the only place God speaks in the whole book of Revelation. We have God's word that it is true.

Exegesis of the Gospel Reading: Matthew 25:1-13

Look, the bridegroom comes. Go out to meet him.

Shortly before Jesus told his disciples this parable, he had also warned them in a whole series of parables about the need to be vigilant. "Therefore, stay awake! For you do not know on which day your Lord will come" (Matt 24:42). He had been telling them that he, the Son of Man, would be coming again. He may be here; he may be there. It will be a time of great tribulation. He told them the story of the fig tree and then of the wise servant. He had been engaged in preparing his disciples with an eschatological discourse, reminding them of the end times. They did not know when the end would come; therefore, they must be watchful.

Now Jesus tells them this parable of the ten virgins. He is continuing the line of instructions he had begun in the previous chapter. Now he uses ten virgins, five wise and five foolish, to illustrate the same thought. All are virgins, all receive the invitation, and all have lamps in their hands. All, however, are not prepared.

The community to which St. Matthew had been writing was divided. Some were looking for the immediate coming of the Lord and some were not. This parable is one of the ways Matthew directed the controversy.

PURPOSE: Each of us has a single goal—to enter the gates of heaven.

SUMMARY: We cannot afford to put off using the means of salvation. They are the special gifts God has put at our disposal. Mary is the most important.

MUSINGS:

1. There is an interesting reference in the preface of this Mass to the east gate of the temple. It refers to Ezekiel 44:2: "The LORD said to me: This gate must remain closed; it must not be opened, and no one should come through it. Because the LORD, the God of Israel, came through it, it must remain closed." It gives us some food for thought.

2. Restoration was the hope of Israel (Isa 9:1-6) and the hope and dream of the followers of Jesus as well. The remembrance of Isaiah nourishes the hope found in this passage of the book of Revelation. Is it with us still?

3. Isaiah lived at a time when conditions in Jerusalem and all Israel were very bad, perhaps the worst in its history until modern times. Still, Isaiah would see a hope, a light, a savior. He had a dream of restoration, of a new Jerusalem from above. It would be filled with dazzling light; it would be refulgent! There the righteous would reside.

4. In the second reading Jesus reminds us that to be late for the promise is a tragedy. Some things cannot be borrowed. The parable

restates yet again the uncertainty of the time of the Parousia and recommends constant alertness.

5. We must take account of the signs of the time, but it will be our readiness, not our calculations, that will bring us to heaven.

6. In our devotion to Mary we have always trusted in her completely. It is a standing joke that when St. Peter turns sinners away, Mary is prepared to receive the sinners by the back door. Only a joke? Whatever. The question is still, are we ready?

RELATION TO THE EUCHARIST: We are to have our lamps lighted in our hands as we approach our heavenly home. Now is the time to trim these lamps.

Sources

Guide for the Christian Assembly: A Background Book of the Mass, 9 vols., ed. Thierry Maertens and Jean Frisque (Notre Dame, IN: Fides Publishers, 1971), IV:162; VI:232; VII:255.

The Jerome Biblical Commentary, ed. Raymond E. Brown, Joseph A. Fitzmyer, and Roland E. Murphy (Englewood Cliffs, NJ: Prentice-Hall, 1968).

The Collegeville Bible Commentary, ed. Dianne Bergant and Robert J. Karris (Collegeville, MN: Liturgical Press, 1989).

INDEX OF SCRIPTURE CITATIONS